THE

SOUL

of the

CORPORATION

⣁ Wharton School Publishing

In the face of accelerating turbulence and change, business leaders and policy makers need new ways of thinking to sustain performance and growth.

Wharton School Publishing offers a trusted source for stimulating ideas from thought leaders who provide new mental models to address changes in strategy, management, and finance. We seek out authors from diverse disciplines with a profound understanding of change and its implications. We offer books and tools that help executives respond to the challenge of change.

Every book and management tool we publish meets quality standards set by The Wharton School of the University of Pennsylvania. Each title is reviewed by the Wharton School Publishing Editorial Board before being given Wharton's seal of approval. This ensures that Wharton publications are timely, relevant, important, conceptually sound or empirically based, and implementable.

To fit our readers' learning preferences, Wharton publications are available in multiple formats, including books, audio, and electronic.

To find out more about our books and management tools, visit us at whartonsp.com and Wharton's executive education site, exceed.wharton.upenn.edu.

THE
SOUL
of the
CORPORATION

HOW TO MANAGE
THE IDENTITY
OF YOUR COMPANY

HAMID BOUCHIKHI | JOHN R. KIMBERLY

Vice President, Publisher: Tim Moore
Associate Publisher and Director of Marketing: Amy Neidlinger
Wharton Editor: Yoram (Jerry) Wind
Acquisitions Editor: Martha Cooley
Editorial Assistant: Pamela Boland
Development Editor: Russ Hall
Digital Marketing Manager: Julie Phifer
Publicist: Amy Fandrei
Marketing Coordinator: Megan Colvin
Cover Designer: Chuti Prasertsita
Managing Editor: Gina Kanouse
Senior Project Editor: Lori Lyons
Copy Editor: Progressive Information Technologies
Proofreader: Gayle Johnson
Indexer: Heather McNeill
Compositor: ContentWorks, Inc.
Manufacturing Buyer: Dan Uhrig

Ⅲ Wharton School Publishing

© 2008 by Pearson Education, Inc.
Publishing as Wharton School Publishing
Upper Saddle River, New Jersey 07458

Wharton School Publishing offers excellent discounts on this book when ordered in quantity for bulk purchases or special sales. For more information, please contact U.S. Corporate and Government Sales, 1-800-382-3419, corpsales@pearsontechgroup.com. For sales outside the U.S., please contact International Sales at international@pearsoned.com.

Company and product names mentioned herein are the trademarks or registered trademarks of their respective owners.

Printed in the United States of America

First Printing September 2007

ISBN 10: 0-13-185726-6
ISBN 13: 978-0-13-185726-1

Pearson Education LTD.
Pearson Education Australia PTY, Limited.
Pearson Education Singapore, Pte. Ltd.
Pearson Education North Asia, Ltd.
Pearson Education Canada, Ltd.
Pearson Educación de Mexico, S.A. de C.V.
Pearson Education—Japan
Pearson Education Malaysia, Pte. Ltd.

Library of Congress Cataloging-in-Publication Data
Bouchikhi, Hamid.
  The soul of the corporation : how to manage the identity of your company / Hamid Bouchikhi, John Kimberly.
     p. cm.
  Includes index.
  ISBN 0-13-185726-6 (hardback : alk. paper) 1. Corporate culture. 2. Corporate image. 3. Brand name products—Management. 4. Business names—Management. I. Kimberly, John R. (John Robert), 1942- II. Title.
  HD58.7.B679 2007
  659.2—dc22
                                                                                    2007020423

*Naima, I look forward to that next chapter
that we will write together.*

—Hamid

*To Barbie, whose faith that long days at the
CNIT would eventually pay off never wavered.*

—John

Contents

x

Acknowledgments

The ideas developed in this book have emerged over many years and, more importantly, owe a great deal to our interactions with numerous colleagues, business leaders, students, and organizations of various sorts, including business firms, hospitals, universities, and churches.

The discussions led by Michel Berry and Jean-Marc Oury of the Paris School of Management inspired our early thinking about the role of identity in business life. Three workshops organized by our colleague David Whetten, of Brigham Young University, in Park City and Sundance reinforced our nascent interest and broadened our understanding of the power and challenges of using identity in the study of management.

Our conversations with Rob Cautilli, Bertrand Collomb, William Kriegel, John Paul MacDuffie, Lisa Reyerson, Jacques Ribourel, and Thérèse Rieul refined our understanding of identity as a multifaceted concept that can be applied usefully to multiple aspects of an organization.

The ideas and frameworks developed in the book carry the mark of our first-hand experience with several companies, including AFAT Voyages, Canal+, Johnson & Johnson, Lafarge, Philips Royal Electronics, Safran Group, SSL International, Wachovia, and Toyota.

Chris Bergonzi, editor of the MIT *Sloan Management Review*, Tim Moore of Pearson Education, and our colleague Jerry Wind of the Wharton School forced us to clarify our thinking and helped us to bring identity out of the academic arena and show how business managers can benefit from mastering what we have come to call the *I*Dimension*.

Scores of students in the MBA courses we teach at Wharton, INSEAD, and ESSEC engaged with us in exploring the souls of the corporations with which they had first-hand experience, as did literally hundreds of participants in various Executive Education programs in which we tested and refined our thinking. We are grateful to them for helping give shape to the *I*Dimension.*

Finally, Martha Cooley, Amy Neidlinger, Russ Hall, Lori Lyons of Pearson Education provided much needed and useful feedback as the manuscript moved toward publication.

Although we are ultimately responsible for the ideas you will encounter in the pages ahead, we continue to be amazed by and grateful for the eagerness of all these individuals and organizations to contribute to the final product. And we look forward to your reactions as well, as we continue to discover ways in which the power of identity can be harnessed in service of improved performance.

About the Authors

Dr. Hamid Bouchikhi is a professor of management and entrepreneurship at ESSEC, a leading European business school based in France. He is interested primarily in the human side of organizations and draws heavily on the social sciences. A native of Morocco who has crossed many geographical and mental borders and collaborated with firms from many parts of the world, Dr. Bouchikhi has developed a sharp awareness of identity and its influence on the conduct of business.

Dr. Bouchikhi's current research topics are in organization theory, corporate entrepreneurship, and managerial innovation, where he has authored and coauthored several books and articles in French and English. His English works have appeared in the *MIT Sloan Management Review*, *Harvard Business Review*, *Organization Science*, *Organization Studies*, *Organization*, and the *European Business Forum*.

Dr. Bouchikhi has been involved with several international public and private-sector organizations through consulting assignments, management development programs, and research projects. He is the founder and academic director of ESSEC Ventures—a center providing training, coaching, logistical support, and seed financing to nascent entrepreneurs in the ESSEC Business School community.

Dr. Bouchikhi has been a visiting professor at Keio University (Tokyo), at the Wharton School (Philadelphia), and at the University of Putra Malaysia (Kuala Lumpur, Malaysia).

Dr. John R. Kimberly is the Henry Bower Professor and Professor of Management, Health Care Systems, and Sociology at the Wharton School of the University of Pennsylvania and Visiting Professor at INSEAD in Fontainebleau, France. He is also Executive Director of Wharton's Global Alliance with INSEAD.

Dr. Kimberly has served as organizational consultant in several organizations in the public and private sectors: the Directorate for Science, Technology, and Industry, and the Directorate for Scientific Affairs of the Organization for Economic Cooperation and Development in Paris, France; the Office of Technology Assessment of the U.S. Congress; the Association of American Medical Colleges, the Robert Wood Johnson Foundation; and the Institute of Medicine of the National Academy of Science. His recent professional leadership activities include membership on the editorial boards of the Academy of Management Review, the British Journal of Management, and M@n@gement. He is the codirector, with Dr. A. Thomas McLellan, of the Center for the Organization and Management of Addiction Treatment, a joint venture between the Treatment Research Institute and the Wharton School that focuses on the business of addiction treatment.

Dr. Kimberly's research areas include organizational design, organizational change, institutional creation, health policy, and managerial innovation. His current projects deal with the content and consequences of firm identity, competition and collaboration among health-care organizations in local markets, the structure and mobility of managerial elites, and competition and change in business education. His most recent book, edited with Hubert Gatignon, was *The INSEAD-Wharton Alliance on Globalizing: Strategies for Building Successful Global Businesses*, published in 2004 by the Cambridge University Press.

He holds a Ph.D. from Cornell University and a BA from Yale University. His previous appointments were at Cornell University, the University of Illinois, and Yale University. He has held visiting appointments at Ecole Polytechnique, France; University of Paris-Dauphine; and Ecole Superieure en Sciences Economiques et Commerciales (ESSEC), Paris. From 1998 to 2002 he was also the Novartis Professor of Healthcare Management, INSEAD, and was responsible for designing and launching INSEAD's Healthcare Management Initiative. He is currently completing a book on the global diffusion of managerial innovation with Professors Gerard de Pouvourville at ESSEC and Tom D'Aunno at INSEAD.

Leadership Challenges in the Age of Identity

Welcome to the Age of Identity. The central premise of this book is that we are in the midst of a transition on a global scale from an era in which the vast majority[1] of individuals and human groups lived with a sense of clarity, continuity, and consistency about their identity—their notion of who they are and how others view them—to an era in which identity is increasingly problematic across all levels of human organization, from the individual person[2] to entire nations or civilizations.[3]

This shift has profound implications for leaders in all walks of life, and particularly in business. To some extent, identity issues and crises in religious, educational, or human service organizations, although potentially highly consequential, are not particularly surprising. These are, after all, organizations that have a strong sense of mission, and as traditional underpinnings shift, you might expect them to be particularly vulnerable to this increasing volatility. You might think that business organizations, with their strong economic orientation and their focus on the bottom line, would be more or less immune to identity questions. Not only is this not the case, but our thesis is that in the Age of Identity, businesses of all kinds are facing identity issues that they do not fully understand and are often ill-equipped to deal with.

The goal of this book is to sensitize you to the central importance of identity in your business and to give you some tools that will enhance your ability to lead in this new context. To set the stage, we highlight ten trends that have characterized the close of the twentieth century and that, together, have created an environment in which organizations of all sorts—businesses, churches, universities, and hospitals—have to cope with essential questions about who they are, who they want to be, and who they can be. Will you be effective as a leader in the Age of Identity? Do you understand the identity issues your business faces? Let's begin with the challenge of globalization.

Globalization

The transition from an environment in which the majority of businesses—especially small and medium-size—were confined to, and often protected in, domestic markets to an environment in which goods, services, and capital flow across borders simultaneously creates new opportunities and poses new challenges. Globalization enables firms to move freely into new markets and geographic areas, but it also brings to the surface questions about who they actually are.

The expansion of McDonald's outside the United States is a particularly good example of the business opportunities and identity challenges that accompany globalization. McDonald's operates the biggest restaurant chain in France and is led by a French management team. The restaurants are owned by French franchisees. Almost all supplies are sourced in France, and the workforce is obviously French. McDonald's France thus has all the attributes of a French organization and is certainly more French than many companies whose products or services are sourced outside of France. And yet McDonald's is widely perceived by French people, and treated by the French media, as an American company spreading "mal bouffe" (the French phrase for junk food) and threatening the French way of life.

In response to a European ban on imports of U.S. hormone-treated beef in 1999, the U.S. government heightened import tariffs on a variety of European products, including *Roquefort* and *foie gras*.[4] Because McDonald's is identified so intimately with the United States, it was subsequently a natural target for the hostility and anger of the French Farmers Confederation, led by the colorful José Bové.

To change the French public perception of the company, the management of McDonald's France launched a massive advertising campaign to stress that it sources 80 percent of its purchasing in France and Europe and that its purchasing power contributes to the welfare of thousands of French farmers.[5] Despite these efforts, the company is still identified with the United States, and the management of McDonald's France has yet to square a difficult circle: persuading the French public that McDonald's France, the organization, is French, although McDonald's, the brand, is American.

The challenges faced by McDonald's as it has expanded globally are hardly unique. The political and psychological resistance encountered by Chinese companies as they enter or make acquisitions in Western markets is the most recent, large-scale illustration of how identity can be a liability. Lenovo, the company that acquired the PC business from IBM, negotiated the right to continue to make and sell PCs under the IBM name for five years[6] after the transaction. However, a firestorm of controversy was created when Lenovo won a contract to supply computers to the U.S. government, with critics raising the specter of threats to data security posed by use of Chinese equipment. In another case, to overcome the liability of "Chineseness," TCL, the second-largest manufacturer of TVs in the world, chose to market consumer electronics gear outside China through well-known Western brands under its full or partial ownership such as RCA, Thomson, and Alcatel.

Although its efforts to acquire the U.S. energy group Uncoal made a splash in the global media village, the China National Off Shore Oil Company (CNOOC) was hindered by its identification with the Chinese government. In an interview with the *Financial Times*[7] a few days after Chevron won the fight for the control of Uncoal, Fu Chengyu, CNOOC's Chairman and Chief Executive, acknowledged that his company failed to change the perception that it was operating on behalf of the Chinese government.

Mergers and Acquisitions

The spectacular growth of corporate mergers and acquisitions in the last quarter of the twentieth century reflects a relatively recent view of firms as commodities that can, and must, be bought, sold, and combined whenever such actions serve the interests of their shareholders. However, the consistently high rates of poor performance of mergers and acquisitions, as documented by dozens of empirical studies, have raised questions about the firm-as-commodity theory.

Although cultural differences are widely cited as a principal factor, little attention has been paid to the more important role of identity. Culture and identity are not synonymous. To illustrate, let's say that two firms with seemingly compatible cultures are merged. Management and employees in both firms value customer orientation, technological innovation, entrepreneurship, value creation for shareholders, and internal cooperation. From a cultural perspective, therefore, post-merger integration should be smooth. At a deeper level, however, we also find that the firms are viewed by their respective members as unique. This sense of uniqueness means that, comparatively, the firms are actually seen as quite different from one another. This view may have been reinforced by several years of intense rivalry between them. Throughout their histories, each of the firms defined its identity, in part, in opposition to the other. The identity of each firm is, to a significant extent, anchored in not being the other. Therefore, despite the fact that their cultures are expressed through similar values, merging them will be a daunting task.

Cultural alignment may mask deeper differences in identity, and for a merger to be successful, managers must find a way to make "one" identity out of "many." Identity integration is achieved when insiders and outsiders "forget" about the identities of the original firms and come to see the result of their combination as a single reality. The challenge of achieving identity integration is dealt with in detail in Chapter 5.

Spin-Offs

The same shareholder value creation logic that has intensified merger and acquisition activity is also behind increasing numbers of corporate spin-offs. Spin-offs, however, have apparently been no more successful than mergers and acquisitions. A study of 232 spin-offs by S&P 500 companies in the 1990s conducted by the Booz Allen & Hamilton consultancy in 2002,[8] for example, revealed that 74 percent underperformed in the stock market. The authors attribute the high rate of failure to suboptimal strategic and financial management of spin-offs. More recent research, however, suggests that performance problems in spin-offs are attributable to more than flawed strategies and financial management practices, and in fact involve identity issues that require proactive management.[9] Even though some spin-offs hit the wall because they were set up to fail,[10] others may fail because the spun-off firm does not develop a viable identity of its own, independent from its former parent. Visteon (Ford) and Delphi (General Motors) are good illustrations of spin-offs where the spun-off companies failed to establish identities of their own, continue to be closely associated with their former parents, and share their destiny. On the other hand, Infineon (formerly a unit of Siemens) and Freescale (formerly a unit of Motorola) were more clearly separated from their former parents at the outset and have, more successfully, established themselves as independent, self-contained organizations. Chapter 6 explores the identity dimension in spin-offs and how managers can help a spun-off company develop an identity of its own.

Disruptive Innovation

The twentieth century ended with a flurry of technological and marketing innovation across major industries: steel, computing, telecommunications, financial services, retailing, health care, and imaging, to cite but a few. In each of these industries, incumbents who thrived on traditional technologies or business models were suddenly attacked by new entrants with very different views of the world—different objectives, strategies, and operating principles. Within the traditional strategic logic, all players are assumed to have access to the same strategic options repertoire, and what separates the winners from the losers is execution. However, this logic misses a significant factor: the way in which identity influences the strategic options that firms consider and implement.

In the steel industry, for example, large integrated steelmakers across the globe used all the strategic weapons at their disposal (consolidation, capacity reduction, exit from commodity low-margin market segments, process innovations) and yet were unable to contain a new breed of steelmakers, the "mini-mills." These mini-mills were built around much smaller and less costly plants and therefore could offer much cheaper prices. For integrated incumbents, it appears that the only effective way to compete against mini-mills would be to become mini-mills themselves or to exit the steel industry altogether. In either case, they would have to radically change who they are. Because changing identity is more difficult than adjusting strategy, large steelmakers have either died (as was the case for Bethlehem Steel[11]), consolidated with other integrated steelmakers to reduce costs and preserve pricing power,[12] or radically redefined themselves (as in the case of the German steel conglomerate Preussag, which morphed into a travel and leisure group [TUI]). What happened in the steel industry also occurred in the computer industry, where the makers of PCs overtook established makers of mainframes and minicomputers. Most of the latter either died (DEC) or reinvented themselves as service providers (IBM and Unisys). In the computer industry, as in the steel industry, identity issues were critical in determining winners and losers. Another example can be found in the imaging industry. Polaroid, at one time the worldwide leader in instant film, collapsed because it was too deeply tied to its conception of itself in instant film.

The examples of IBM and TUI show that disruptive innovation does not necessarily lead to the destruction of incumbent firms. Survival depends on the ability of senior management of the incumbent to sense when an innovation is potentially disruptive and to put their firm through the deep and often painful changes required to succeed in the new era. Those who fail to perceive the magnitude of the disruption and who fail to understand the inertial character of identity put the future of their firm at great risk.

Deregulation

Sparked by the realization that state ownership and monopolies tend to inhibit competition, innovation, consumer choice, and cost effectiveness, the recent wave of deregulation and privatization around the globe has been highly disruptive for many established firms and their sense of themselves. As these efforts unfolded, many incumbent organizations, with identities forged under monopolistic conditions, found it difficult to compete effectively. Deregulation enabled the entry of new competitors with superior marketing, technological, operating, and managerial prowess and forced incumbents to face fundamental identity questions. A few industries that have been hit by massive deregulation include electricity, transportation, banking, and telecommunications. Companies that have successfully adapted to the new competitive environment were able to make the transition, more or less quickly, from thinking of themselves as monopolies serving the public good to viewing themselves as businesses that have to compete for the hearts and minds of customers on the basis of superior value propositions.

The threats to long-established monopolies posed by deregulation are well illustrated by the examples of AT&T in the United States and Electricité de France (EDF) in France. In the ten years following the 1996 federal deregulation act, AT&T went through several gut-wrenching strategic and operational changes aimed at defining a new AT&T. Although repeated downsizing, numerous reorganizations, and various investments, divestments, and spin-offs under Robert Allen (Chairman and CEO of AT&T from 1988 to 1997) raised hopes, AT&T did not find new life. Despite being hailed as an outstanding choice to replace an embattled Allen in 1997, Michael Armstrong was no more successful at establishing a viable identity for AT&T. After two good years in which AT&T's stock was carried to incredible heights by the dot-com tide, Armstrong witnessed the free fall of the stock price (see Figure 1), a trend that continued under his successor, David Dorman, who took the helm in 2002. In an ironic turn of events, AT&T was eventually swallowed by SBC, one of the Baby Bells forced out of its corporate family by the telecommunications act.

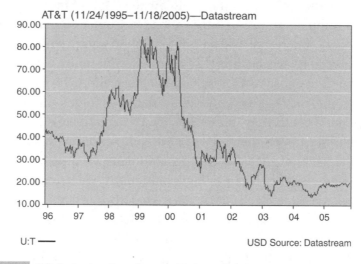

AT&T (11/24/1995–11/18/2005)—Datastream

U:T —   USD Source: Datastream

Figure 1 AT&T stock price after the Federal Deregulation Act

The challenges faced by EDF, the French electricity monopoly, provide another good example. The deregulation of electricity production and distribution in the European Union compelled the French government to open the domestic market for competition and to privatize EDF. However, the transition of EDF from a monopoly to a free-market player provoked numerous strikes and protests orchestrated by labor unions and leftist political parties. Although the center-right government led by Dominique de Villepin floated a portion of EDF shares on the Paris stock market in 2005, a law passed in 2004 does not allow the government to own less than 70 percent of the shares and voting rights in EDF. As a result, EDF today is neither a private company nor a public-sector organization. Furthermore, the ambiguity about the identity of EDF has exposed France to criticism from other European countries for several reasons:

- The French former monopoly is seen as behaving as a free-market player abroad, where it has made many investments and acquisitions[13] thanks to easy access to state aid and government-guaranteed borrowings.

- At the same time, however, electricity distribution is still a monopoly in France, and it is still difficult for a non-French competitor to enter the domestic market.

- It is impossible, by law, for a foreign investor to acquire a significant stake in EDF.

In contrast with EDF, which is still struggling to shed its public-sector identity and to embrace a free-market-based identity, other European companies such as BT (the former British Telecom) and Air France have successfully completed their metamorphoses and are leaders in global, highly competitive industries.

Strategic Alliances, Organizational Networks, and Boundaryless Organizations

The evolution in many industries from integrated, self-sufficient firms to networks of interdependent organizations blurs organizational boundaries and brings identity issues to the forefront. The typical biotechnology firm, for example, draws its revenue from partnerships with several big pharmaceutical companies that require strict firewalls to be erected between projects and teams to protect their investment. In the automobile and electronics sectors, the adoption of lean manufacturing with its zero inventory and just-in-time systems has led suppliers to build dedicated units and organizations on clients' assembly sites. A similar evolution is observable in information technology services, where outsourcing means that service providers build dedicated, permanent units with their own management structure on clients' premises.

People who operate in these new, "boundaryless" organizational contexts are often unclear about who their employer really is and where their loyalty must lie. When much of a firm's competitive advantage resides in the knowledge, skills, and commitment of its workforce, leaders must ensure that employees have no doubt who their employer is. And herein lies a major challenge. Although they have to open the firm's strategic, operational, and physical boundaries to enable close collaboration with multiple partners, managers must also erect thick *psychological* boundaries and build a distinctive organizational identity that people can identify with and feel loyal to regardless of who they work with on a daily basis or where they work from. The paradoxical demands of networks are taken to an extreme in virtual organizations. The more virtual an organization is, the more it must rely on psychological processes to create and maintain a sense of togetherness and belonging among employees who operate in multiple workplaces and time zones.

Chapter 7 elaborates further on identity issues in the specific context of strategic alliances that may or may not require the creation of a separate organization.

A Society of Organizations

A hallmark of the Age of Identity is the increased prevalence of organizations everywhere in society.[14] Organizations are involved in every aspect of our existence, from birth to death.

In traditional societies, individuals inherited much of their own identity from the social milieu (family, place of birth, tribe, religion) into which they were born. In an organizational society, individuals are defined by the organizations in which they participate. The firm, therefore, is no longer just a workplace but a socially and emotionally loaded entity. The firm has become, perhaps unintentionally, a supplier of individual and collective identities. This evolution brings new demands and responsibilities to management. When employees, and often other stakeholders, draw much of their sense of self from belonging to, or buying from, a particular organization, they tend to be anxious about and resist changes that may alter what, in their eyes, is the very soul of that organization.

Because they did not appreciate the significance of identity, the trustees of the Milton Hershey School Trust were surprised and overwhelmed by hostile reactions to the proposed sale of the trust's holdings in the Hershey Company (formerly Hershey Foods and Co.) in the summer of 2002. The trust owned 31.4 percent of Hershey's outstanding common shares and 76 percent of voting rights,[15] and it intended to diversify its holdings. At the time, analysts estimated that competition among potential buyers, including Nestlé, Kraft Foods, and Cadbury Schweppes, could lift Hershey Foods' price tag to as much as $12 billion.[16]

The decision to put Hershey Foods up for sale provoked a hostile chain reaction that took the trustees by surprise. Opposition to the sale came from many quarters: employees, residents, former trustees, high-profile alumni of the Milton Hershey School, judges, the Pennsylvania Attorney General, and the state's lawmakers. All feared that the sale of Hershey Foods to one of its major competitors not only would endanger 3,000 jobs but would also betray the legacy left by Milton Hershey, who dedicated his life to using business for the pursuit of common good. After two months of fierce fights in the courts and in the media, the trustees conceded defeat and declared that the trust's share of Hershey Foods was no longer for sale. You can get a sense of the depth of people's feelings about the sale in the following excerpt from a *Fortune* magazine story by John Helyar:[17]

Late that night a resistance leader named Bruce McKinney got the news (of the canceled sale) at home. He went outside and clanged a bell to wake his neighbors with the glad tidings. They came out to dance and drink in front of the DERAIL THE SALE signs that lined the street. It was like V-J Day in Chocolatetown Square the next morning, with citizens whooping and drivers honking.

The townspeople, you see, felt they hadn't just saved an estimated 3,000 jobs; they had reclaimed their legacy. Hershey is one of the last company towns in America in an age when most have gone the way of the nickel candy bar. But Hershey is much more than that. It's a unique place where company, community, and charity intertwine in a remarkable century-long social experiment.

The conflict surrounding the proposed sale reflected diverging definitions of Hershey Foods. To the trustees, Hershey Foods was a business that could be bought and sold as any other. They did not see the business as central to the philanthropic mission of the Hershey Trust. On the opposite side, employees, residents, and Milton Hershey school alumni viewed Hershey Foods as more than just a business and emphasized its centrality to the "social experiment" initiated by Milton Hershey and to the identity of the community that grew around the chocolate business.

Although the cool-headed analyst may have been appalled by the rejection of the price offered by Wrigley and Nestlé for the company's stock, people who drew their sense of identity and community from the company were more sensitive to a different calculus. To them, Hershey Foods was a central institution in their lives and thus could not be bought and sold as though it were a commodity.

To avoid the complications faced by the Hershey trustees, leaders must understand when a change initiative is likely to alter the essence of the organization in the eyes of key stakeholders. Leaders who pursue this sort of change must be prepared and able to deal with collective psychological and emotional phenomena that are very different in nature and implications from mechanical calculations of value creation.

Reputation and Accountability

In a society in which who makes a product has become as important as, if not more important than, the intrinsic characteristics of the product itself, leaders must ensure consistency between the firm's view of itself and how it is viewed in the outside world. Inconsistencies in these views will inevitably lead to problems.

A good example of the detrimental effects of misalignment between a firm's sense of itself and how it is perceived externally is the widely publicized controversy in which Degussa, a German chemical company, found itself embroiled during the construction of the Holocaust Memorial in Berlin.

After a TV documentary revealed that Degussa had owned Degesch,[18] the firm that supplied the Zyklon-B used by the Nazis in extermination camps, the foundation overseeing the construction of the "Memorial to the Murdered Jews of Europe" voted against using an anti-graffiti coating made by Degussa to protect the thousands of concrete slabs erected in memory of Holocaust victims.[19] The 22-to-1 vote by the foundation's trustees came after weeks of heated public debate and reflected the view, held by the trustees and a wide section of the general public, that the Degussa of 2003 was the same as the company that owned the maker of the deadly gas six decades before.

The trustees' decision came under criticism from many circles. In an interview with the German newspaper *Tagesspiegel*, Avi

Primor, the former Israeli ambassador to Germany, saw no rational reason for excluding Degussa from construction of the Memorial and added that "Degussa today has nothing to do with the Degussa of the Nazi era."[20] Peter Eisenman, a U.S. architect with a Jewish background, was less diplomatic. He criticized the decision as "political correctness" and said that "Germans today should not all continue to be held responsible for the actions of their parents."[21] In an interview[22] with National Public Radio (NPR), he added, "I think (the trustee's decision) is allowing us to be held hostage to history. And, you know, had I thought that this was an issue, I would never have gone into this project in the first place."

How should top management react to a potentially damaging crisis they neither provoked nor anticipated? Should they argue that equating Degussa with the Nazi Era was unfounded, or accept it? Dismissing the equivalence could be seen as additional evidence of the company's guilt. Accepting it, on the other hand, could upset employees and other stakeholders and threaten their identification with the company. The company's statement, made the day following the trustee's decision, shows how fine a line the company's leadership had to walk:[23]

Degussa is aware of the past of its predecessor companies. Chairman Prof. Utz-Hellmuth Felcht comments: "Actively working through and coming to terms with the history of our company is a matter of central concern for us." ... Moreover, Degussa is one of the founding members of the "Remembrance, Responsibility and Future" Foundation...Today's Degussa Group employs a workforce of 48,000 worldwide—of all religions, including members of the Jewish faith. It is no easy matter to explain to the employees why they are facing this decision, given that they know about the history and also how the *"new"* [our emphasis] Degussa is actively working through and coming to terms with it.

This statement shows that the company's leadership was aware that a rational, analytical reaction to the crisis would not be appropriate in a highly charged emotional context. The chairman did not seek to challenge the identification between the old and the new Degussa on rational grounds. Instead, he empathized with those who felt offended by the company's involvement in the Memorial and sought, at the same time, to reassure employees by stressing the "new," guilt-free Degussa.

The decision to change the company name of the well-known cigarette manufacturer Philip Morris to Altria illustrates a different—and, in our view, less effective—handling of identity in a context where accountability and reputation issues occupy a central place in a firm's life. As the tobacco industry came under attack almost everywhere across the globe, the management of Philip Morris adopted a new name, hoping to reduce the company's exposure to negative comments. This kind of maneuver can buy time, but its effects will not last long, because the company remains committed to cigarette manufacturing and the high margins it provides. Altria will continue to be perceived, internally and externally, as a cigarette company and will continue to be held accountable for the consequences of its behavior. To change its public perception and reduce its accountability, Altria would have to go through genuine identity change, either by exiting the tobacco industry altogether or, at least, inventing a radically different, less controversial, way of making and selling cigarettes.[24]

The Advent of Alternative Social Identities in the Workplace

In the industrial age, workers were grouped and managed within occupational categories represented by unions in collective bargaining processes with management. Individuals belonging to the same occupational category received the same rights and were subject to the same obligations.

The decay of this model over the past few decades is persuasively argued by Michael Piore of the Massachusetts

Institute of Technology (MIT) and his colleague Sean Safford of the University of Chicago in an article published in a recent issue of the journal *Industrial Relations*:[25]

> Under the New Deal era of collective bargaining, the broader storyline—the one with which workers ultimately identified—presumed the Weberian distinction between the rational economic realm and the irrational social realm...It is impossible in today's world to imagine one's work career without incorporating one's social context into it: that is, such aspects of life as parenthood, health, and the social stigma that may attach to one's race, religion, or gender.... Social identity, in this context, serves as a ready alternative to a work-centered plot and, therefore, to work identities as an axis of mobilization. (p. 319)

The trends encapsulated in this quote from Piore and Safford entail new challenges for management and labor unions. The interpenetration of social and economic spheres enables multiple social identities to be carried into the workplace. These social identities put new claims on management for recognition and tailored treatment and challenge the foundations of occupational-based labor unions. In the Age of Identity, business leaders need to be alert to and manage the identity of the organizations they are entrusted with. At the same time, they are increasingly under pressure to acknowledge and respond to the manifold social identities carried into the workplace or projected onto the organization by outside groups.

The Self-Aware, Empowered Consumer

The salience of multiple identities within the workforce is paralleled by increased self-awareness among consumers for whom buying and consumption decisions are becoming occasions for expressing, asserting, and reinforcing personal and social identities. Even though the share of "identity-based" consumption is still low, it is growing and will inevitably challenge mainstream suppliers of products and services to reckon with the identities of customers who feel increasingly empowered as a result of the following factors:

- The availability of products and services that are explicitly designed to fit with their self-identity
- The availability of real-time information on competing products and their suppliers
- The availability of opportunities to communicate instantly with other members of their reference groups

To cope effectively with this trend, managers need to master "identity marketing."[26] Consider, for example, the challenges posed to Coca-Cola and PepsiCo by the rapid growth of Mecca Cola, a soda launched in France in 2002 by a Tunisian-born lawyer. The militant founder wanted to offer French Muslims an alternative to Coke and Pepsi, pledging, in the process, to give 10 percent of the profits to Palestinian charities and another 10 percent to charitable works in Europe.

As long as the new soda was not available through mainstream French retail channels and could be bought only in ethnic stores, the market leaders, Coca-Cola and PepsiCo, did not need to worry about its popularity within a small consumer segment that identifies strongly with its militant agenda. But the swift international expansion of Mecca Cola can no longer be ignored by established competitors. The company recently relocated its headquarters to Dubai, in the Middle East, and is building a large industrial complex. The company is now marketing a range of soft drinks in 64 countries and sold 1 billion liters worldwide in 2005.[27] The founder boasts that Mecca Cola has become the third-world brand for cola after Coca-Cola and Pepsi.[28]

The success of Mecca Cola and the proliferation of other militant soda brands have forced Coca-Cola and PepsiCo to reconsider their marketing and advertising strategies in Arab and Muslim countries. In a story commenting on the legacy of former Coca-Cola Chairman and CEO Douglas Daft, the *Financial Times* wrote:[29]

Mr. Daft also consciously played down Coca-Cola's American image. Its Coke brand has been a particular target for Muslims fighting against perceived American imperialism. Several private cola brands, including Mecca Cola, have emerged in the region to challenge Coke's business. Now the company has adopted a "think local, act local" mantra throughout its sales and marketing teams. Rather than depend on the Atlanta headquarters to create one advertising theme, Coca-Cola's local offices create commercials tailored to local tastes and sensibilities.

In addition to producing local commercials, Coca-Cola is said to counter Mecca Cola's assaults through pricing power, credit facilities, and other weapons that its size and economies of scale afford it. Will this be enough? The long-term answer will depend on how deep and how long the new competitors will be able to capitalize on Arab-Muslim self-awareness and turn consumers away from established brands by merely presenting themselves as ethnically compatible Arab-Muslim products.

Our view is that Coca-Cola and PepsiCo and other mainstream businesses threatened by identity-based competition must learn how to compete on this new terrain. Commercials featuring local faces are a step in the right direction, but this may not be enough. To cope effectively with identity-based competition, mainstream players must consider launching brands anchored in the same identity or react on the basis of alternative desirable identities. To Coca-Cola and PepsiCo, the first strategy means working with local business partners to launch brands that can make comparable, though less radical, identity claims and that will have easier access to technologies, marketing expertise, and mainstream retailing channels. The second strategy means competing on the basis of alternative social identities within the

Arab Muslim world. One can think, for example, of brands that would appeal to women or to the large section of the population that thinks of itself as modern but feels equally distant from radical nationalistic, often fundamentalist, claims and Western lifestyles.

The Pervasiveness of Branding

Because traditional references and labels are losing their effectiveness in defining individuals, organizations, and even countries, a focus on branding has become a central feature of the Age of Identity. In business, the need for effective branding is compounded by intensifying competition between firms offering increasingly comparable products and services. In this context, the identity of the firm that makes and stands behind a product or service is becoming as important as the intrinsic attributes of that product or service.[30] Corporate branding, a fast-growing activity, enables leaders to use the firm's identity as competitive weapon. In addition to competitive differentiation, leaders use corporate branding to position the firm favorably vis-à-vis its stakeholders: current or prospective employees, investors, analysts, journalists, or activist groups. Business leaders who are attracted to corporate branding should know, however, that corporate branding is a double-edged sword and can sometimes make them easy targets for adverse activist groups. The following quote from an article published by Naomi Klein in *The New Statesman* captures the paradox of branding:[31]

I doubt this current surge of anti-corporate activism would have been possible without the mania for branding. Branding, as we have seen, has taken a fairly straightforward relationship between buyer and seller and—through the quest to turn brands into media providers, art producers, town squares and social philosophers— transformed it into something much more intimate. But the more successful this project is, the more vulnerable these companies become to the brand boomerang. If brands are indeed intimately entangled with our culture and identity, then, when they do wrong, their crimes are not easily dismissed as another corporation trying to make a buck. Instead, many of the people who inhabit these branded worlds feel complicit in their wrongs, both guilty and connected. And this connection is a volatile one, akin to the relationship of fan and celebrity: emotionally intense but shallow enough to turn on a dime.

If you are tempted to use the identity of your firm as a basis for competitive advantage, you need to be aware of some common risks and pitfalls:

1. Be sure that the organizational identity projected through branding efforts is real. If it is not real, if it is mere sloganeering, your competitors, or other unfriendly stakeholders, may turn these branding efforts against you. Failure to observe this rule exposed the British Petroleum Company (BP) and its top management to a storm of criticism after an explosion at the Texas City, Texas, refinery in 2005, where 15 workers lost their lives. The following quote[32] provides a good illustration of how BP management's presentations of BP as a "green" and socially responsible company are being used against it in the media:

Another day, another battering for BP. The final report from the US Chemical Safety Board on the Texas City refinery explosion in 2005 made some pretty unpleasant reading for the UK supermajor, which prides itself on corporate social responsibility. Men working 29 days of continuous 12-hour shifts, as was highlighted in the review, sits uneasily with claims of a safety-first regime. Many of the report's findings have been aired before and BP "strongly disagrees" with some of the conclusions, but the tragedy in which 15 people died has been one major wake-up call—both for BP and the industry.

2. Ensure the consistency of corporate branding efforts targeted at various stakeholders. The risk in adapting each message to its recipients is that multiple, and sometimes conflicting, images may be projected, leading to confusion in the marketplace.

3. Carefully align your own behavior and decisions with the organizational identity claims you make inside and outside the firm.

4. Strive to realize synergies between handling identity at the level of the organization as a whole and at the level of the individual brands under which your firm's products and services are marketed. Chapter 8 deals with this topic in more detail and suggests managerial strategies for maximizing synergies between organizational and brand identities.

This introduction highlighted a number of trends that together constitute significant challenges for firms doing business in the Age of Identity—challenges that confront leaders of these firms with tough questions about the essence of the organizations for which they have responsibility. Although these trends represent different and, *a priori*, unrelated phenomena, they have one thing in common: They are about changes in the business environment that leaders cannot respond to by merely adjusting business strategies or operating systems and routines. To respond effectively to these changes, leaders have to reach much deeper, to the firm's identity, and determine whether it is an asset they can leverage to bring about change (as you will see in Chapter 2) or a liability they must address to avoid being obliterated by new competitors (as discussed in Chapter 3). To assess how much of an asset or liability your firm's identity might be, you first need to know precisely what identity is. So read on.

Endnotes

1. Although uncertainty about the identities of some individuals and groups is probably as old as mankind, it must be stressed that identity used to be problematic only for individuals and, often oppressed or suppressed, minorities in societies whose mainstream had little doubt about collective and individual identity.

2. The British sociologist Anthony Giddens discusses issues of individual identity in late modernity. His arguments are developed in *Modernity and Self-Identity*, a book published in 1991 by Stanford University Press. Richard Sennett elaborates on the same phenomena in his popular book *The Corrosion of Character: The Personal Consequences of Work in the New Capitalism* (1998, W.W. Norton & Company).

3. An insightful discussion of these identity issues in the twenty-first century can be found in two books by Samuel Huntington: *The Clash of Civilizations* (1997, Simon & Schuster) and *Who Are We? America's Great Debate* (2004, Simon & Schuster).

4. *Dow Jones Business News,* August 31, 1999: "French Farmers Protest Against McDonald's, U.S. Trade Sanctions."

5. *La Tribune,* August 20, 1999: "McDonald's France achète 80% de ses produits agricoles dans l'Hexagone."

6. *Financial Times,* November 9, 2005: "Anatomy of a Deal."

7. *Financial Times,* November 8, 2005: "CNOOC Bloodied but Unbowed."

8. Lucier, C., J. Dyer, and G. Adolph. 2002. "Breaking Up Is Hard to Do—and to Manage." *Strategy+Business,* 28:1–4.

9. Corley, K.G. and D.A. Gioia. 2004. "Identity Ambiguity and Change in the Wake of a Corporate Spin-Off." *Administrative Science Quarterly.* 49:173–208.

10. This is the case of spin-offs for which the main motive is to rid the parent company of a doomed business unit or to clean its balance sheet.

11. Bethlehem Steel was liquidated in 2003 after selling industrial assets to International Steel.

12. The combination of Arcelor and Mittal Steel is a perfect illustration of this path. Arcelor was formed by merging the French Usinor with the Spanish Arceleria and the Belgian Arbed. Mittal Steel grew through successive acquisitions and consolidations of ailing steelmakers in Eastern Europe and the United States.

13. In Europe, EDF made full acquisitions or bought significant stakes in electricity utilities in Germany, Hungary, Italy, Poland, Spain, and the United Kingdom. EDF is also actively involved in Africa, in the

Americas, and in Asia. In 2004, EDF generated $17.5 billion in revenue (out of $47 billion) outside France and $4 billion (out of $12 billion) in earnings before interest, taxes, depreciation, and amortization (EBITDA). Source: The EDF Group, *Annual Report,* 2004.

14. The advent of a society of organizations was first articulated by William Whyte in his classic book, *The Organization Man* (1956, Anchor Books). For a more recent discussion of the role of organizations in society, see Perrow, Charles. 1991. "A Society of Organizations." *Theory and Society,* 20:725–762.

15. The *Wall Street Journal,* July 25, 2002: "Sweet Deal: Hershey Foods Is Considering a Plan to Put Itself Up for Sale."

16. Dow Jones News Service, August 7, 2002: "Hershey School Group Requests Lawmakers to Stay Any Sale."

17. *Fortune* magazine, October 14, 2002: "Sweet Surrender. There Was Much Rejoicing When the Town Founded by Milton Hershey Blocked the Sale of His Chocolate Company. But Was It Really a Victory?"

18. Degussa owned, until 1986, a 42.2 percent share in Degesch, which delivered Zyklon-B cyanide tablets to the Nazis for use in the death camps' gas chambers.

19. *Western Daily Press,* October 27, 2003: "Holocaust Firm Banned."

20. *Agence France Presse,* October 29, 2003: "L'architecte du mémorial de l'Holocauste soutient le groupe chimique Degussa."

21. *Agence France Presse,* November 5, 2003: "Nazi-Linked Firm Helped Build Holocaust Memorial Foundation."

22. NPR Radio, October 31, 2003: *All Things Considered.*

23. Degussa company press release, October 28, 2003.

24. Ways to change public perception may include inventing a nicotine-free cigarette, or allocating a large portion of the profits to a charitable foundation dedicated to cofunding health care for heavy smokers, among other options.

25. Piore, M., and S. Safford. 2006. "Changing Regimes of Workplace Governance, Shifting Axis of Mobilization, and the Challenge to Industrial Relations Theory." *Industrial Relations,* 45:299–325.

26. For a discussion of identity marketing, see Reed II, Americus, and Lisa Bolton. 2005. "The Complexity of Identity." *MIT Sloan Management Review*, 46/3:18–22.

27. *FOOD,* May 24, 2005: "'Mecca Cola': A Sign of the Times."

28. Mecca Cola company Web site (www.mecca-cola.com), accessed March 20, 2007.

29. The *Financial Times,* March 10, 2004: Wall Street is convinced that Steven Heyer, the company's president and chief operating officer, is the man for the top job. But the board is conducting an unprecedented external search, and some believe Heyer has other goals.

30. On the benefits and approach to corporate branding, see Aaker, David A. 2004. "Leveraging the Corporate Brand." *California Management Review*, 46/3:6–18.

31. Klein, Naomi. 2000. "The Tyranny of the Brands." *The New Statesman,* 129/4470:25–28.

32. Upstream: "BP living dangerously," March 23, 2007.

The *I*Dimension*

What is the ***I*Dimension***, and why should managers care about
it? To answer this question, we need look no further than that
quintessentially American icon, the Coca-Cola Company. The
company has been losing ground to Pepsico since the untimely
death of charismatic CEO Roberto Goizueta in 1997; its
shareholders have been unhappy, some quite vocally so, about
its performance. According to a story written by *Fortune*
magazine reporter Betsy Morris[1] about the company's 2006
Annual Meeting, Neville Isdell, the current CEO, told an
audience of more than 400 shareholders the following:

Next month the Coca-Cola Company will celebrate its 120th
anniversary—120 years since someone paid a nickel for Doc
Pemberton's inspiration-in-a-glass at Jacobs Pharmacy. Today
consumers invite us into their lives more than a billion times a day
for enjoyment, fun, and refreshment. We understand, however, that
what has sustained us these first 12 decades will not be sufficient
for the future.

According to Morris, Isdell described how senior management and the board had concluded that they would not diversify away from beverages and would focus on becoming a nonalcoholic beverage company with an expanded range of product offerings aimed specifically at meeting consumer needs. She went on to write: "That may not sound like much, but for Coke it's what Isdell calls a 'revolutionary evolution.'"

And indeed, in May 2007 the company announced its intent to acquire Glaceau, a producer of vitamin-enhanced water, for a staggering $4.1 billion. Even this acquisition, however, may not be enough to reestablish the company's dominance. Andrew Martin wrote in the *New York Times*[2] shortly after the announcement:

The Glaceau deal is a milestone for a company that has never pulled off a takeover of this magnitude before. Even so, some analysts still wonder whether Mr. Isdell and his board remain too conservative to break from traditions that once served them well but may no longer be suited to a world in which consumer tastes are rapidly— sometimes constantly—shifting.

As you will see later in this chapter, Isdell and his team were struggling with what we call the *I**Dimension and its consequences. They were wrestling with the question of how much the Coca-Cola Co. could change and still be the same. They were wondering whether their historical reliance—first on a single beverage, Coke, and subsequently on an expanded line of beverages—would be sufficient to maintain their viability as a company.

On the surface, it appears that Isdell and his team were dealing with issues of strategy, and indeed this is how they may have framed their discussions. But we see it differently. To us, they were dealing with fundamental identity questions: Who are we as a company? How do our customers see us? To what extent will our identity enable us to thrive in the future? The answers to these questions have strategic implications, to be sure, but they come from something deeper in the company. They come from the company's identity, from the more or less shared perception about its essence by those inside and outside the firm. As you will see, identity can be a real asset and a source of great strength, but it can also become a liability and a source of potentially fatal weakness.

This chapter provides a conceptual framework that helps you think about and deal with identity issues. To this end, we open the identity "black box" and look at the *I*Dimension* from several complementary angles. We explore how a firm's identity is both related to and different from other notions, such as organizational culture, brand positioning, and reputation. We also show how managing the *I*Dimension* implies balancing daily a set of inevitable and contradictory tensions at work.

The *I*Dimension*

When we examine an organization from the outside, we see a given ownership and governance structure, products, technologies, business strategies, organizational structures, systems, policies, operating rules, employee characteristics, and perhaps a publicly articulated set of values and beliefs. In an ideal world, these elements would fit well with and reinforce one another (see Figure 1.1), leading to acceptable levels of performance. When a firm's performance is not satisfactory, the conventional view would suggest that the problem lies in misalignment in one or several of these elements and would recommend that steps be taken to produce realignment.

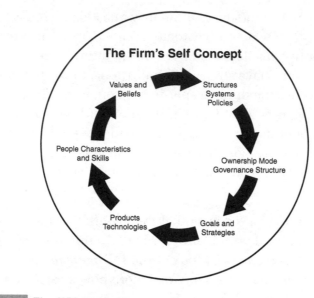

Figure 1.1 The *I*Dimension*

We take a different view in this book. We argue that the visible elements of a firm are held together by a set of shared beliefs—sometimes implicit, sometimes explicit—that define its essence. This set of shared beliefs—what we call the ***I*Dimension***—gives the visible elements of the firm coherence and puts boundaries around how much change is possible without altering its essence. As the Coke example illustrates, the ***I*Dimension*** typically lies in the collective unconsciousness of stakeholders, because organizations, like most individuals, have a natural tendency to take their identity for granted and to go on with their daily business without wondering who they are, if they are satisfied with who they are, or who they should or want to be. A "normal" life, for an organization or individual, is not possible without assuming that identity is, at least temporarily, settled. This is an assumption that enables one to cope with ongoing opportunities, questions, and challenges within an unquestioned sense of self. However, there are times when conflicting views among stakeholders make an organization's identity problematic. This is what is happening, for example, in many modern universities. Some stakeholders are committed to a view of the university as an organization dedicated to knowledge production and dissemination. Others view it as a business that should be driven by competitive and budget considerations. When identity becomes problematic, leaders need to understand that they are confronting issues beyond strategy and that invariably involve struggles over the soul of their organization. When these issues arise, leaders need to understand how the identity of their organization is anchored and what the implications may be.

Identity Anchors

Just as the identity of individuals can be anchored in gender, nationality, social group, educational credentials, or particular skills, an organization's identity, its *I*Dimension,* resides in multiple anchors, such as core business, knowledge base, nationality, operating philosophy, a legendary founder, a governance structure, or combinations of these.

Any aspect that key stakeholders (employees, owners, suppliers, customers, bankers, shareholders) view as core, enduring, and distinctive[3] about an organization is part of its identity. The weighting and salience of different identity anchors may vary considerably from one organization to another. For example, technological innovation is more central to the identity of Apple than it is to McDonald's. Nationality defines Toyota, internally and externally, more than it defines Google. And the mayhem provoked by its proposed sale, in the summer of 2002, revealed that ownership and governance structures are more central to Hershey Foods than they are to the identities of Nestlé or Cadbury Schweppes. The weight and salience of identity anchors can also vary over time for the same organization. Until the rumors swelled, in the summer of 2005, about a possible takeover by Pepsi Co., the national identity of Danone went unnoticed. The hostile reaction of unions and French political leaders to Pepsi's overtures reminded the world that Danone was a French icon and that the government would do everything in its power to prevent it from falling into the hands of an American giant.[4] This episode shows that, in normal times, identity anchors lie deep in collective unconsciousness, are typically taken for granted, and generally are not subject to open discussion. Identity anchors are brought to the surface by unusual events or circumstances that compel some stakeholders to ask "Who are we?" or "Who are they?"

Identity anchors reflect subjective, though shared, beliefs about an organization's essential characteristics. This means that two organizations founded in the same geographical and cultural area, in the same period of time, and in the same industry can have their identities anchored in very different dimensions. HP and Intel are good examples. While much of HP's historical identity was rooted in a particular way of doing business, the famous HP way, Intel's identity is summed up in the "Leap Ahead" creed and is vested in technological innovation.[5]

The Tensions: Identity as Partly Designed and Partly Emergent

An organization's identity emerges early in its life through the conscious, or unconscious, decisions and choices made by founders and managers about the key aspects of the new organization: choice of industry, strategy, technology, organization, people, competitive position, and product mix, to name only the most obvious.

Ben & Jerry's, Apple, The Body Shop, Bang & Olufsen, Southwest Airlines, and W.L. Gore are examples of companies whose identities were to a great extent designed by their founders to carry and reflect their own orientations and value systems. However, most companies develop unique identities as they grow and cope with various issues in the process of conducting their business. The unique ways in which these issues are approached come to form a pattern that makes the company easily recognizable by internal and external stakeholders. For example, innovation had not been at the core of 3M in its early years as a mining venture until it ran into severe performance problems. Innovation became a defining and distinctive aspect of the company only when its founders moved into manufacturing to escape a looming bankruptcy.[6] Microsoft became a PC software giant almost by accident after Bill Gates' encounter with the team behind IBM's venture in the PC business in the early 1980s. Merck became an independent U.S. corporation in 1917 after the federal government seized the German company's assets in the United States during World War I.

When a firm's identity is deliberately defined by its founders, it is explicitly articulated in the form of a corporate identity statement, a mission statement, or a set of values, principles, or ways of doing things. In firms that develop an identity as they grow, identity typically remains tacit and unnoticed. In these firms, awareness of identity and the need to articulate it explicitly usually grow as the firm has to deal with unusual events (such as a hostile takeover), as it is challenged by massive change in its environment (deregulation or a new technology), or as its management drives it in a new direction (such as internationalization).

The Tensions: Internal and External Identity

Because it defines how an individual or organization stands apart from other entities, identity entails a tacit negotiation between the focal individual or organization and other individuals or organizations. In other words, an individual's identity is not a private matter; it is a social construction. To illustrate, I am free to think of myself as I wish, but my definition of myself would be problematic, and I would be at risk of an identity crisis, if the people around me did not validate my self-definition. For example, I can think of myself as a woman, but people around me keep seeing me as a man. I can think of myself as a great tennis champion, but my friends would keep reminding me of my mediocre performance on the court.

By analogy, a firm's identity is formed but not unilaterally decided on by its founders, managers, or members. Sometimes, the external world (customers, investors, competitors, journalists, government) validates the proposed identity, as was the case for Southwest Airlines. In other cases, the outside world resists the identity sought by the founders for their organization. In the early years of Apple, Steve Jobs defined his upstart as a universal alternative to IBM. But the reality of the PC industry told him that Apple could not be more than a cool niche player.

The negotiated character of identity helps us understand how identity is different from culture, although the two concepts are often confounded. An organization produces its culture (a set of values and beliefs) through internal processes, while an organization acquires its identity through repeated exposure to and interactions with the outside world. With no other organization to be compared to, as is the case of isolated tribes, an organization cannot and does not have to develop an identity. Inevitably, however, it develops a set of values, beliefs, and norms to guide the behavior of its members vis-á-vis each other.

Balancing a firm's theory of itself with how it is viewed externally is a key managerial challenge, because a healthy life is impossible without some alignment between how members (owners, employees, managers) view their firm and how it is viewed by relevant external constituencies. Every business leader should ponder the issues stirred by the hostile takeover of Arcelor[7] by Mittal Steel.[8] The takeover was resisted, in the European countries where Arcelor is a significant employer, on the grounds that Mittal Steel was a hungry Indian company eager to swallow a European jewel only to close European plants and transfer jobs to low-cost countries. In an effort to correct the public perception, Lakshmi Mittal, the founding owner-manager, emphasized that Mittal Steel, too, was European. He stressed that the firm is managed from London, is incorporated in the Netherlands, owns several plants in Eastern Europe, and has no manufacturing base in and no business ties with India. To signal his goodwill, Lakshmi Mittal went as far as promising to keep jobs in Europe, to make room for Arcelor's top managers and significant owners in the new management and governance structure, and to establish the merged company in Luxembourg, where Arcelor was headquartered. And yet, in the emotionally charged atmosphere provoked by his initiative, all the explaining and concessions did not help change the public correlation of Lakshmi's Indian background and citizenship with the identity of the global steel leader he grew in three decades outside India. Had Lakshmi Mittal been more sensitive to the *I*Dimension,* he would have first designed a public campaign around the corporate identity of Mittal Steel to establish it as a European company, in the eyes and minds of European stakeholders, before launching a hostile takeover of Arcelor. His initiative would still have been met with resistance from incumbent management and some labor unions, as is always the case in hostile bids, but the resistance would have found less support in the general public and among politicians. More importantly, it would have been easier for Lakshmi Mittal to entice Arcelor's individual and institutional shareholders—among them its most important shareholder, the Luxemburg government, which owned 5 percent—to accept his offer. He would have been able to focus his energy on the deal, not on explaining the "true" identity of Mittal Steel.

The Tensions: Sameness and Uniqueness

Although the dominant discourse about corporate identity and branding tends to overemphasize identity as that which conveys an organization's uniqueness, social identity theorists[9] remind us that identity also serves to categorize individuals and organizations. A clear identity indicates the category in which an individual or organization belongs and, at the same time, communicates how the individual or the organization stands apart from peers.

The need to know where an organization belongs is of equal importance to an organization's internal and external constituencies. For example, physicians cannot be recruited or retained by an employer if they do not recognize it as a health-care provider. Stock analysts are confused when they are uncertain about which known category a given firm belongs to and reflect their confusion in unfavorable valuations.

Examples of companies that are both easily recognizable as members of a category and unique among their peers are numerous. Toyota is an automaker that is very different from all other carmakers. McKinsey is a consulting firm and unique among its peers. Wegmans is a supermarket chain and stands apart among its competitors. How can Toyota, McKinsey, and Wegmans be easily recognizable as members of a given industry and unique at the same time? The answer is that their identities are anchored in aspects that make them look like other members of their category (automaking, consulting, and retailing) and in other aspects that differentiate them among their peers (consistent commitment to a unique manufacturing system for Toyota, to advice to top management for McKinsey, and to a distinctive management philosophy for the privately held U.S. retailer Wegmans).

The categorizing and differentiating functions of identity show identity management in a new light. Corporate identity and branding experts urge managers to differentiate their company, which is certainly crucial in an economy where customers, investors, and skilled employees are solicited by multiple competitors. If managers pursue differentiation too far, however, they may blur the organization's membership in established, legitimate categories. The managers of the British Royal Mail paid dearly for ignoring this aspect of identity. In their enthusiasm to position the soon-to-be-privatized organization as a major player in the new logistics and supply-chain-management era, they named it *Consignia* and gave it a grand mission statement:

We are trusted to connect every person, business and community in the UK...through outstanding personal service, based on the skills, pride and commitment of everyone who works in Consignia.[10]

The organization's constituencies were told that the post office was no longer what they had always known as the Royal Mail. However, Consignia, still operating mail collection and delivery while diversifying in new businesses, could not possibly be considered a courier company like UPS, FedEx, and DHL. To end the confusion, management had to ditch Consignia and give back to the organization its old Royal Mail name and identity.

Good identity management requires subtle balancing of markers of sameness and uniqueness to allow stakeholders to come up with easy answers to "What kind of company is this?" and "How is this company different from all others of its kind?"

The Tensions: Convergence and Divergence

Organizations differ on how much consensus there is among their key constituencies about their identity. The attempted sale of Hershey Foods in the summer of 2002 revealed a conflict between the trustees of the Milton Hershey School Trust and other stakeholders on the essence of the company. The trustees viewed Hershey Foods as a business that could be traded and thought that the philanthropic mission resided in the Trust, not in the business. Members of the community disagreed and argued that the social mission was integral to the identity of Hershey Foods.

Leaders who are sensitive to the *I*Dimension* focus on where and how to drive a company to high convergence among key stakeholders about its essence. The identity of Bang & Olufsen, the Danish consumer electronics company, is anchored in using cool designs to offer well-off customers a distinctive entertainment experience and pieces of furniture they are proud to show in their living rooms. The company's clear and consensual identity allows the management team to focus, for example, on the kinds of products they should make, the kinds of customers they should target, how the products are to be sold, and how many resources are to be invested in design and after sales. When the company experienced serious performance problems in 1991, the management team leaned on the company's identity to devise a recovery plan that allowed better implementation and, at the same time, reaffirmed the firm's historical identity.[11]

As long as identity is in harmony with the firm's industry and with the wider environment, it is a very effective compass for management. By contrast, firms whose identities are contested continually among key stakeholders are much more difficult to manage. In these organizations, even mundane decisions can trigger passionate debates about the soul of the organization. The current controversy about the future of the Public Broadcasting System (PBS) illustrates what happens when an organization's identity is disputed. In this case, the conflict is between those who believe that public broadcasting should favor quality programming over market share and those who argue that it should secure its own funding by appealing to a wider audience through less elitist programming. The terms of the debate were summed up by Joseph Weber of *Business Week* in an article[12] titled "Public TV's Identity Crisis: Can PBS Reach New Viewers and Still Stay PBS?" Other organizations whose identity disputes have become publicly visible include the BBC[13] and New York City museums.[14]

An obvious implication of this discussion is that you should strive to foster consensus among key stakeholders about the identity of their firm. Less obvious but no less important, however, is that you should not try to eradicate divergence. Extreme convergence in an organization's identity brings about narcissism and insulation from the outside world. Hence, instead of pushing for convergence and eradicating divergence, leaders who understand the significance of identity should strive to maintain some tension between the two forces to achieve the minimum of consensus without which collective action is impossible, and the minimum of dissent without which change is impossible.

The Tensions: Aggregation and Fragmentation

In their seminal book, *Organization and Environment,* Lawrence and Lorsch[15] argued that effective management requires the balancing of structural differentiation and integration. The following elaboration about identity fragmentation and aggregation comes close to Lawrence and Lorsch's thinking but deals with a different set of phenomena. Fragmentation refers to the process by which identities emerge at different levels of an organization as it grows larger and more complex. Identities can emerge at the level of work groups, departments, business units, geographic entities, subsidiaries, and so forth. Aggregation refers to the process by which subunits are glued together by the feeling of belonging to a common whole. In contrast to structural differentiation and integration, which are managerially driven, fragmentation and aggregation are social psychological processes that managers can try to influence but cannot design.

Organizations vary regarding the way in which the balance between forces of aggregation and fragmentation is struck. At McKinsey, IKEA, and Apple Computers, the identity of the whole clearly outweighs local identities. No matter where they are based in the world, employees of these organizations identify strongly with the parent company. In other instances, commonly found among firms that grow through acquisitions, fragmentation outweighs aggregation. Employees in these firms tend to identify more with subunits than with the parent company. We observed this scenario in a large French multinational company that used to conduct an annual employee survey in its affiliates worldwide. The survey consistently showed that while employees in Europe and emerging countries identified strongly with the French parent, North Americans tended to identify more with their local subsidiary.

The levels of identity aggregation or fragmentation have practical consequences. Firms with highly aggregated identities enjoy a high level of cohesion among their members, which enables smooth communications, coordination, common purpose, concessions, and even sacrifice in difficult times. Organizations with a highly fragmented identity lack the psychological glue that binds people together across and above subunits. Managers in these settings have to work much harder to align local strategies and behaviors with those of the parent company, because they cannot rely on a shared sense of identity to ensure the alignment.

The average manager today is well equipped to balance global and local strategies and to design differentiated and integrated organizational structures. But the majority of managers lack awareness of, and the skills to influence, identity aggregation and fragmentation in their firms. To have a chance to influence these processes, you should first understand and accept that fragmentation is inevitable and responds to the need of human beings to create small categories where they can belong and with which they can easily identify. Aggregation, although crucial to an organization's effectiveness, is less natural and requires significant energy from management to counter fragmentation. Identity aggregation can be pursued through various means, ranging from symbolic initiatives (a corporate identity statement) to substantive processes (moving people across business units, functional domains, and countries to reinforce company-wide *esprit de corps*). We consider various approaches to identity management in more detail in Chapter 11, "Strategies for Leading in the Age of Identity."

Balancing Contradictory Tensions in Identity

The foregoing discussion highlights the fact that the identity of an organization is intrinsically and inevitably subject to multiple and conflicting tensions (see Figure 1.2). These tensions are inevitable because identity is open-ended and can never be considered an aspect that is set once and for all for an organization. The tensions are contradictory because they push the firm in opposing directions. Instead of seeking to suppress contradictory tensions, managers must balance them and ensure that their firm's identity is not pushed too far, and for too long, on any of the dimensions discussed previously. A firm whose identity is insulated from the outside world is set for autism. Conversely, a firm whose identity is defined from the outside never develops a distinctive personality. Too much emphasis on uniqueness can harm a firm's legitimacy, because outsiders cannot see to which category it belongs. Reciprocally, too much eagerness to look like other legitimate members in a given category leads to loss of character. Too much convergence does not allow healthy appraisal of a firm's identity in the light of evolving circumstances, but too much divergence leads to paralysis. Finally, too much fragmentation threatens internal cohesion and identification with a collective self, while too much emphasis on aggregation favors cloning and turns away the individuals and groups who do not accept seeing their self-identities melded in an overly homogeneous organizational identity mold.

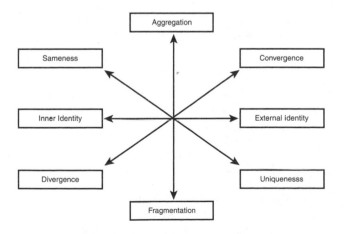

Figure 1.2 Balancing contradictory tensions in the *I**Dimension*

When these tensions are balanced appropriately, and when there is reasonable consensus among stakeholders about an organization's identity, it can be an amazing asset, as you will see in the next chapter. If the power of identity is underestimated or ignored, however, or if too high a premium is placed on convergence and consensus, it can become a serious liability. It can threaten not only the job security of senior management, but also the future of the organization, as you will see in Chapter 3, "The Dark Side of the *I*Dimension*." Where do you think your organization is in the *I*Dimensional* space?

Endnotes

1. *Fortune* magazine, May 15, 2006: "Coke gets a Jolt. The soft drink giant has done business the same way for 120 years. Now CEO Neville Isdell wants it to face the future."

2. The *New York Times*, 27 May 2007: "Coke Struggles to Keep up with Nimble Rivals."

3. Albert, S., and D. Whetten. 1985. "Organizational Identity," in Cummings, L.L., and B.M. Staw (eds.). *Research in Organizational Behavior*. Greenwich, CT: JAI Press, 263–295.

4. *Financial Times*, July 23, 2005: "The Ironies of French Resistance to PepsiCo's Advances."

5. The centrality of technological innovation to Intel's identity is explicit in the following introduction of the company on the corporate Web site: "Intel, the world leader in silicon innovation, develops technologies, products, and initiatives to continually advance how people work and live. Explore the many ways Intel's belief in innovation has defined our corporate identity" (www.intel.com/intel/index.htm).

6. "A Century of Innovation: The 3M Story." www.3M.com.

7. The number-two steelmaker in the world until the takeover by Mittal Steel, Arcelor was formed, in 2002, by the merger of the French Usinor with the Luxembourg-Belgian Arbed and the Spanish Arceleria.

8. Mittal Steel is the global leader in the steel industry. It grew to this position through acquisitions and effective turnaround of underperforming operations throughout Eastern Europe, Asia, North America, and Latin America.

9. Tajfel, H., and J.C. Turner, 1985. "The Social Identity Theory of Intergroup Behavior," in Worchel, S., and W.G. Austin (eds.). *Psychology of Intergroup Relations*, 2nd ed. Chicago, IL: Nelson-Hall, 7–24.

10. *The Guardian,* January 23, 2002.

11. Ravasi, David. "Bang & Olufsen A/S." European Case Clearing House: 305-056-1.

12. *Business Week,* September 30, 2002, p. 65.

13. *The Guardian,* November 25, 1992: "Battle of Air Waves Creates Identity Crisis."

14. The *New York Times,* July 11, 2004: "New York's Bizarre Museum Moment."

15. Lawrence, P., and J. Lorsch. 1967. *Organization and Environment.* Cambridge, MA: Harvard University Press.

The Bright Side of the *I*Dimension*

Think of companies as diverse as IKEA, The Body Shop, Bang & Olufsen, Harley-Davidson, Southwest Airlines, Starbucks, Ben & Jerry's, McKinsey, W.L. Gore, and Toyota. All operate in intensely competitive markets through increasingly commoditized products or services. Yet all are enduring global leaders in their respective industries. Unsurprisingly, these companies, and many others that share the same attributes, have generated a great amount of interest among managers, consultants, journalists, and management researchers. The "secret" of their enduring market leadership and economic performance has been explored in hundreds of books, articles, and case studies. This activity has created a "market" of business success factors where the products, or theories of success, are profoundly marked by the disciplinary or professional backgrounds of their authors: strategic innovation, superior execution, progressive human resources management, effective knowledge management, customer relationships management, smart branding, charismatic leadership, cohesive organizational culture, lean manufacturing, and efficient supply-chain management, to name only a few.

Although each of these factors can be found in one or more of the companies in the preceding list, none by itself captures the whole picture. Take the example of Southwest Airlines. Does it owe its success to its low-cost business model, to the way it targets particular geographic markets and routes, to its branding and marketing strategy, to its people-oriented human resources management, to its fun culture, or to the personality of its founder? The answer is probably all of the above.

Now think of Toyota. Does it owe its success to the much praised and copied lean manufacturing system, to its volume-driven strategy, to its obsession with quality, to its Japanese roots, to its emphasis on job design and training, to its brand management, to its tight management of distribution channels, or to its human resources management system? Again, the answer is all of the above, enveloped in the legendary "Toyota Way."

This exercise can be repeated endlessly, but you can see where we are heading. The success of these firms is not to be found in single factors but in the way all dimensions of the firm are held together and mutually support one another. In other words, success is systemic and lies deeper than its superficial manifestations. If it were otherwise, many competitors would have been able to imitate and supersede Toyota, IKEA, Starbucks, McKinsey, or Southwest Airlines.

These companies have remained out of the reach of their competitors because during several decades of consistent behavior vis-à-vis their internal and external constituencies, they have acquired a unique and enduring identity that sets them apart from their competitors and makes them difficult to imitate. For example, many Western managers have learned that Toyota's lean manufacturing model is not easy to emulate because it is part of a system that goes beyond manufacturing. You can copy Toyota's manufacturing model, but you cannot copy the special status the firm has acquired in the eyes of its employees, customers, suppliers, distributors, and investors.

The examples mentioned here suggest that as technologies and industries mature, and as products and services become increasingly comparable, sustainable competitive advantage cannot be built on easy-to-imitate business strategies or operating systems. The more comparable products and services are, the more managers will have to build competitive advantage on inimitable attributes of the firm or, we contend, its identity.

In the remainder of this chapter, we explain in more detail how identity can be an enduring, hard-to-imitate source of competitive advantage by exploring the internal and external benefits of clear and consistent identities.

The Internal Benefits of Clear, Consistent, and Valued Identities

Identification

People who work for companies that have a clear, consistent, and valued identity are easily induced to identify strongly with their employer and to draw a significant part of their personal identity from the firm. The beneficial by-products of strong identification are many. Employees draw a feeling of pride from belonging to a particular organization and are encouraged to project a positive image of the organization to the outside world. An organization that enjoys strong identification among its employees has many ambassadors and advocates and needs less help from PR (public relations) experts to project a positive company image.

W.L. Gore, the company that invented the GoreTex fabric, has no advertising or corporate branding budget. Yet, the firm has enjoyed a great amount of positive free publicity thanks to its consistent ranking at the top of the "Best Companies to Work for" in the United States and Europe.[1] Why should the managers of W.L. Gore spend money to promote the company when it is so well promoted by its employees?

On the opposite side, firms with an unclear, inconsistent, or socially problematic identity cannot enjoy positive identification from their employees and may even suffer from deliberate efforts of their members to distance their self-identity from that of their employer. These firms cannot fully engage the hearts and souls of their employees and have to invest time and resources in promoting themselves to not only external but also internal constituencies.

Loyalty and Commitment

Organizations with a clear and valued identity inspire feelings of loyalty and commitment among their employees because their consistency fosters trust and reliability. The behavioral manifestations of loyalty and commitment are multiple and beneficial. Loyal employees are less easily lured away from their employer by other employers for a higher salary. Hence, the firm can invest confidently in the development of its people's technical and managerial skills. Loyal employees are also mindful of the interests of their firm without being guided or constrained to do so. Loyal employees can make concessions and sacrifices more easily when the company faces difficulties. For example, to help Southwest Airlines[2] cope with the difficulties challenging the airline industry, the unions made salary concessions without going through the usual labor/management arm-twisting so characteristic of the U.S. airline industry.

Cooperation

When employees at all levels identify with and have a strong sense of belonging to the same organization, management needs to spend less time and energy designing and enforcing formal systems and procedures of cooperation. The sense of common destiny and the willingness to preserve the interests of the organization provide natural incentives for cooperation. The strength of the organization's identity works as insurance against the emergence of parochial ways of thinking and doing that are so common in organizations with highly fragmented identities.

A Guide for Problem Solving and Decision Making

A clear and consistent organizational identity provides employees with a framework for decision making and problem solving. Because managers cannot and should not specify how employees should make decisions in every possible circumstance, a clear organizational identity is an effective guide for dealing with problems and decisions. For example, the centrality of the environment and social responsibility theme in the identity of the Body Shop sets clear boundaries regarding which strategic and operational decisions can be made by employees in different roles and capacities throughout the organization.

People who have a clear understanding of and agreement with their firm's identity do not need to be told what they should do in particular circumstances. The answers lie in their interpretation of their company's soul.

Legitimacy

Because managing a firm requires establishing priorities and sometimes making tough decisions, the perceived legitimacy of priorities and decisions is vital to their acceptance and implementation. In this respect, companies that have a clear, consistent, and socially valued identity worry less than others about the legitimacy of their managers and the decisions they make for the organization. The managers are promoted on the basis of their identification with the organization and embody it.

The legitimacy of their decisions is unquestioned because their decisions are aligned with the firm's established identity.

The External Benefits of Clear, Consistent, and Socially Valued Identities

The external benefits of identity are not fundamentally different from those that are primarily internal, and the two are mutually reinforcing.

Recognition

In an economy where many competitors offer comparable products and services, it is important for firms to make themselves easily recognizable to customers, prospective employees, investors, and opinion makers. Companies such as Starbucks, IKEA, and The Body Shop have achieved high levels of external recognition through a unique combination of physical aspects (design of outlets, visual identity), product selection, marketing strategies, and corporate values. Bang & Olufsen has distinguished itself from all other makers of consumer electronics through consistent emphasis on design, careful management of the brand and the distribution network, and projecting to the outside world its unique philosophy and management practices (relaxed working atmosphere, care of its people).

A firm that enjoys a high level of recognition thanks to a unique and valued identity does not need to promote itself in the usual ways to relevant constituencies.

Attractiveness and Loyalty

A clear and positive identity acts as a magnet for employees, customers, investors, and other business partners who are attracted to deal with the firm. The process creates a sort of halo effect and enables the firm to build a loyal audience in the circles whose input it needs for its survival and growth. For example, when it has achieved a high level of external recognition, it is much easier for the firm to attract new talent.

Trust and Predictability

With a consistent identity, a firm can nurture a feeling of trust among its employees, customers, and investors. Employees know who their employer is and do not fear overnight changes in corporate goals, strategies, and management practices. Customers come to and keep buying from the firm because they trust it and expect it to stand behind its products and services. Investors support and remain loyal to the company because they perceive it as reliable and predictable.

The Virtuous Cycle

The firms mentioned in the opening of the chapter have all achieved a high level of clarity and consistency between their internal and external identity. These companies are taken in a virtuous cycle where external reputation fuels internal pride and vice versa. The question now is whether managers can proactively shape the identity of their firm and create the kind of virtuous cycle enjoyed by the likes of Starbucks or Southwest Airlines. The short answer is that managers can shape the identity of their organization to a significant extent if they keep in mind that identities, individual or collective, can never be entirely specified and unilaterally engineered. We reserve the development of this argument for Chapter 11, "Strategies for Leading in the Age of Identity." We invite you to see, in the next chapter, the different ways in which a firm's identity can be a major liability rather than a decisive competitive asset.

Endnotes

1. For the eighth consecutive year, W.L. Gore & Associates, Inc. earned a position on *Fortune's* annual list of the U.S. "100 Best Companies to Work For."

Gore ranks second overall and first among midsized companies in the magazine's January 24, 2005, issue. For the second year in a row, Gore–U.K. ranked No. 1 among the "100 Best Places to Work in the U.K." (2005).

Gore–Germany is ranked in the Top 10 in the overall ranking and No. 5 in midsized companies among the "50 Best Places to Work in Germany" (2005).

In 2004 Gore–Italy ranked in the Top 20 among the "35 Best Places to Work in Italy" (2004). Source: W.L. Gore & Associates company Web site, www.gore.com/en_xx/.

2. Southwest Airlines obtained salary concessions from its unions.

The Dark Side of the *I*Dimension*

Do you remember Digital Equipment Corporation (DEC)? This company challenged IBM's supremacy with minicomputers that occupied less space, were less expensive, and were easier to operate than IBM mainframes. At the height of its glory in the 1970s, DEC was seen by many as a daring innovator poised to take over Big Blue and lead the world computer industry. Fast-forward to 1998, and you see a struggling DEC being swallowed by a conquering Compaq[1] that planned, as a starter, to slash 15,000 of DEC's 53,500 jobs. Fast-forward again to 2007, and DEC no longer exists. It has disappeared both as an organization and as a brand. The consistent, enduring, and distinctive identity that served DEC so well in the 1960s and 1970s became a trap from which it was unable to escape.

As the example of DEC so clearly illustrates, the multiple benefits of a consistent, distinctive, and enduring identity—its bright side—can become liabilities if top management is unwilling or unable to see beyond issues of strategy and operations and appreciate its potential dark side. To help managers cope with the dark side of identity, this chapter pinpoints a number of common dysfunctions and suggests ways to address them.

Narcissism

As with individuals, organizations are prone to narcissism. Organizations fall into narcissism when their owners, employees, and key stakeholders converge around a clear and consistent identity for the organization, draw pride from belonging to or dealing with the organization, and remain committed to their definition of the organization despite signals, weak or strong, that the organization's identity may no longer be adequate or viable.

To illustrate, let's go back to the DEC story. Many observers and management scholars have glossed over the case and put forward several explanations as to how the company came to such a sad ending. Harvard Professor Clayton Christensen contends that DEC, like many other technology firms, failed because it did not predict the disruptive change introduced by the pioneers of personal computing.[2] This theory is plausible and can be applied successfully to many other cases. However, the disruptive change theory does not offer a convincing explanation as to why many firms fail to predict, or most of the time just acknowledge, disruptive technological innovation.

To get to the roots of a firm's failure to foresee and adapt to change, we need to leave the realm of economics and strategy and consider the relationships between identity and performance. When a firm is perceived as successful, its stakeholders are led to attribute good performance to some inner attributes of the organization. In the process, they increase their commitment to the organization as it is. The narcissistic loop is reinforced as more success brings about more faith in and commitment to the identity of the organization. At extreme levels of narcissism, organizations become inward-looking and shut down adverse feedback channels.

Organizational self-absorption is not specific to the technology sector. Moulinex, the French maker of small appliances, fell victim to the same syndrome that failed DEC. Moulinex was founded in the aftermath of World War II by Jean Mantelet, a self-taught engineer. Mantelet had a simple yet strong vision: offer French households innovative, quality kitchen appliances at a moderate price and create as many jobs as possible in France. To achieve his vision, Mantelet built an organization where growth, innovation, cost leadership, and job creation formed the core of its identity. As a result of Mantelet's vision and the unique organizational identity he defined for the organization, Moulinex enjoyed several decades of continuous international growth and profitability. In the process, the company developed a sense of itself—confirmed by external perceptions—as a leading, innovative French industrial company. This self-concept did not enable Moulinex and its stakeholders to cope with a changing environment in the early 1980s—market saturation in Western countries and new competition from low-cost Asian countries. Despite growing adversarial evidence, Jean Mantelet, his loyal management team, and the employees were unable to think of Moulinex as something other than a highly successful small-appliance company with a strong French industrial base.[3] Their inability to challenge the company's deep-seated identity ultimately led to its liquidation in 2002.

Managers can help their firms avoid chronic narcissism by maintaining feedback channels and forcing internal and external stakeholders to acknowledge dissonant information from the environment. Louis Gerstner will long be remembered for forcing IBM to admit that it was no longer the sole rainmaker in the information technology (IT) sector[4] and broadening its self-concept beyond mainframes.

Identity Conflict

Identity conflict occurs when influential stakeholders hold, and are committed to, competing, equally clear, and mutually exclusive views of the soul of the same organization. As a result, the firm is continuously torn between conflicting objectives, business strategies, and operating principles.

A good example of identity conflict can be seen in the Catholic Church. The election of Pope Benedict XVI brought into the spotlight a set of issues that have been tearing apart the Catholic Church for many years and that bear profound consequences for the perennial identity of the Church. Reformists, worried about the decline of the Church in Western societies, urge adaptation to life in modern societies by abolishing the obligation of celibacy for priests, allowing the ordination of women, and taking a more inclusive attitude on birth control and homosexuality. Conservatives, on the opposite side, contend that the "Laws of God" are immutable and that the Catholic Church should not align itself with society when it deviates from the Laws of God. The debate between the reformists and the conservatives conveys deep conflict about the very essence of the Catholic Church. The conservatives agree that the Church would likely gain more followers and priests if it took a softer stand on societal issues but object that the Catholic Church would lose its essence. Reformists believe the contrary. The Catholic Church would lose its essence as the House of God if it failed to live in the world and did not engage with humanity as it is.

Conflict about identity is a common fact of business life, even though it may not involve as many emotions as is the case for the Catholic Church. In the business world, Jacques Nasser's forced departure from Ford Motor Company revealed a deep conflict between the historical emphasis on car manufacturing in Ford's identity and the consumer-oriented service company promoted by Nasser:[5]

At the start of last year we reconfirmed our commitment to being the world's leading consumer company for automotive products and services. Our vision makes customers the foundation of everything we do and superior shareholder returns the ultimate measure of our success. When you view your business from the customer's perspective, you shift from a "transaction" mentality to a "relationship" headset—from merely selling a vehicle to providing an ongoing stream of automotive-related products and services that suit a customer's needs over a lifetime.

The conflict between Nasser's view and other stakeholders' views of Ford (employees and unions) was eventually resolved when the Ford family stepped in, ousted Nasser, and put Bill Ford at the helm of the organization. Nasser's ousting and his replacement with Bill Ford signaled, internally and externally, that Ford was going back to its industrial roots and emphasis on making products. Bill Ford made this clear in the first annual report following the transition at the helm of the company:[6]

One of the great advantages we've always had is that we're not another nameless, faceless corporation. The Ford family involvement has given the Company a special relationship with the people who work here. Our dealer and supplier partners also are part of our extended family. Many of them have been with us since the beginning and have been a part of the Ford success story.

In 2001, we lost focus on the critical elements of products and people. It cost us dearly. But difficult times provide an opportunity to re-examine core values and to take bold action. We have done both. In November of last year we put a product-focused leadership team with a proven record of strong results in place.

Reasserting its historic identity, however, was not enough to get Ford back on track. Bill Ford was replaced as CEO by Al Mulally in the fall of 2006.

The decision to put Hershey Foods up for sale revealed, in a different way, conflicting understandings of the firm's identity. The Hershey Fund trustees viewed Hershey Foods as a typical business that could be sold without consequences for Hershey's social mission, because the social mission formally resides at the level of the Trust, not the firm. On the opposite side, the employees and the local community viewed the ownership of Hershey Foods by the Hershey Trust as integral to its identity.

The battle between the management of Nestlé, the Swiss food conglomerate, and the employees of Perrier is another illustration of how bitter the conflict about identity can get. The managers of Nestlé are promoting the idea that Perrier is a water brand that is not necessarily tied to Vergeze, France, the location of the spring used to fill Perrier bottles. Fearing that this theory of Perrier might mean fewer jobs and investment in Vergeze, unions and local politicians have been lobbying the European Union (EU) Commission for a general ruling about "place of origin" that would prohibit Nestlé from bottling Perrier elsewhere.[7] As can be seen in the following quote from the daily newspaper *Le Figaro,* the theory linking the essence of Perrier to Vergeze found sympathetic ears and advocates in the French government:

The French industry minister, Patrick Devedjian, said yesterday that Perrier mineral water is geographically specific in that it comes from springs in Vergeze in southeastern France. Speaking in the French senate, the minister claimed that, if Perrier's owner, the Swiss food giant Nestlé, decided to sell water from other springs under the Perrier brand, consumers would not be fooled. Mr Devedjian also acknowledged, however, that Perrier is not legally linked to the Vergeze site.

Managers can cope with identity conflict either by maintaining a workable balance between the present forces or by clearly favoring one view of the firm. Contrary to a widely held opinion, conflict is not necessarily a bad thing. After all, it is common for different parties to hold somewhat different views of the same organization. Furthermore, the presence within the same organization of different views of its identity can enable it to present itself in different ways at different times to different constituencies. The question, then, is a matter of degree. As long as conflicting views of the organization do not generate confusion, paralysis, or a high level of detrimental infighting, managers should not be overly worried by lack of consensus on the essence of the firm.

When conflict about the identity of the organization reaches a threatening level, managers should support the view of the organization that they see as the most viable. For example, one part of the management team of a British multinational company viewed the firm as a participant in the health-care industry, while another viewed it as a consumer products company. Although it was softly expressed, the conflict about the firm's identity went along with questions about where and how the company should pursue future growth. To settle the matter, the CEO articulated a clear vision of the company as a maker of "branded consumer products distributed through retailing channels." To enforce the company's new identity, the CEO divested all the businesses that did not fit with the company's new definition, regardless of their performance.

Drift

Drift occurs when an organization with a clear and consistent identity progressively loses focus and its original sense of self. Drift settles in and often goes unnoticed. It usually happens when managers develop new activities, enter new markets, acquire other firms, and involuntarily blur the clarity and consistency of the firm's identity. Kmart and Boeing are good illustrations of gradual drift. In its efforts to challenge Wal-Mart's supremacy and to sell everything to everyone, Kmart ended up with a blurred identity and became synonymous with persisting poor performance. When the board of directors appointed James B. Adamson to bring the company back from Chapter 11, he was very articulate, in an interview given to *Business Week,* about the need to first clarify Kmart's identity:

One of the key things we have to decide is, should we carry a little bit of everything for everybody, or do we really have to be more dominant in categories the customers are coming to us for? And that we have to answer very quickly...*The issue is: Who is Kmart?* I want to take the time and figure it out, and analyze the research, what our store managers are saying, what our employees are saying about why do customers come to Kmart? Where do we let down? And what are our strengths? Because as you go through that process, which is going to be an exhaustive process, it affects every tentacle of this company. We already have exclusive brands within our company. We already have a presence in the urban market. We have pieces, but the issue is how do they all fit together, and what makes sense going forward?[8]

Boeing is another case of a large corporation experiencing an identity drift. In its efforts to "distance (Boeing) from its identity as just an aircraft company,"[9] management moved corporate headquarters to Chicago, away from its historical base in Seattle, and engaged Boeing in major projects far from its historical core business in civil and military aviation. Among other initiatives, Boeing worked on a program to revolutionize the nation's air traffic control system by deploying satellites and extended a plan to distribute movies to theaters via satellite. These projects did not materialize,[10] and the company has been taking one hit after another: revelation of corrupt practices in the defense contracting business, the threat of losing leadership in civil aviation to Airbus, and an embarrassing affair between former Chairman and CEO Harry Stonecipher and a female employee. The net result of the process is that Boeing is no longer the civil aircraft manufacturer that it used to be, but it is still hard to figure out what the new Boeing is.

Managers can cope with drift by working to clarify the firm's identity. They can, for example, put an end to drift by reaffirming the organization's historical identity. Steve Jobs' comeback at the helm of Apple has reconciled the company with its historical identity anchored in innovation and design. Apple almost sank under Jobs' predecessors' efforts to make it into a me-too maker of PC gear without the necessary volume and cost structure to compete against IBM, Dell, or Compaq. Managers can reconcile a firm with its historical identity by divesting recent acquisitions, by refocusing on its traditional markets and customers, or, in extreme cases, by changing its ownership structure to give the founders, or the guardians of its philosophy, more weight in governance and decision making. This approach is no guarantee of success, however, as the case of Ford illustrates.

The opposite strategy for treating drift is to articulate clearly a new identity for the firm and to pursue its implementation forcefully and consistently. This is exactly what Jean-Marie Messier did for former Compagnie Générale des Eaux—a water distribution company that had become a hodgepodge of more-or-less related businesses ranging from telecommunications, book and magazine publishing, real estate, private hospitals, and cable TV to waste management and electricity generation. To end the confusion generated by decades of frantic diversification, Messier articulated a vision for Vivendi as a global media and communications company and sought to align its portfolio, business strategies, and operations accordingly. As we will show in the next chapter, however, the difficulties encountered by Messier in executing the new vision for Vivendi suggest that revolutionary identity change is a risky proposition.

Fragmentation

Organizations experience identity fragmentation when individuals and groups come to identify more with subunits than with the organization as a whole. When this occurs, the bonds between employees and the organization as a whole are weakened. The typical consequences of high levels of fragmentation are a loss of common purpose and mutual support across units and the firm's inability to deal with and to be recognized by its environment as a single organization. In a French multinational company, North American employees continued to identify with their local affiliate for several years, and in some cases several decades, after the acquisition of their business by the French parent. As a result, the French side complained about the Americans' lack of loyalty and commitment to the "group," while Americans felt that the French parent was too remote geographically and culturally and looked like an exclusive club. The psychic divide has very concrete consequences. North Americans resented coordinating their strategies (such as competitive pricing) with their European partners and minimized their involvement in global strategic initiatives decided at the Parisian headquarters.

Fragmentation is dysfunctional when local identities come into open or tacit conflict with the established identity of the organization and may, in extreme cases, provoke schism. Although schism is more frequent in faith- or ideologically based organizations, it is also observable in business life. The circumstances leading to the creation of St. Luke's, a leading British advertising agency, are a good illustration of schismatic fragmentation. The company was founded in 1995 after Andy Law, manager of the London branch of the Chiat/Day advertising agency, and his colleagues rebelled against the sale of the parent company to Omnicom, which merged it with TBWA. The London team felt betrayed and could not identify with the new parent they were told to join. Instead of complying with Jay Chiat's order to facilitate the merger of the UK operations, Andy Law led a rebellion and persuaded his colleagues to work with him to create an organization that would better reflect their "quest" for independence and equality. After much arm-twisting with corporate headquarters, Law and his colleagues were able to buy out the London office and establish St. Luke's. The company they built is equally owned and governed by its employees following the "one man, one voice" principle and is driven by the quest for independence, creativity, and fun.[11]

Managers should understand and accept that some level of fragmentation is inevitable and corresponds to the universal tendency of human beings to identify with their immediate work or social groups. Every individual draws his or her identity from several groupings and layers of social organization. The same individual can view him- or herself as a mother or father, as a lawyer, and as an American without necessarily experiencing these identities as conflicting or inconsistent. To enable multiple identities to thrive within the same organization, leaders must ensure that the different identity layers present in their firm complement and fit well with each other so that the same employee can identify with a professional community, with a business unit, and with the overall company, and yet experience these identities as mutually supportive. Managers should balance fragmentation and aggregation, promoting and protecting local identities when necessary, and reinforcing a common identity to maintain a feeling of togetherness and being part of the same project.

Like fragmentation, narcissism is inevitable and necessary. Every organization meets challenges—from its competitors, customers, investors, or regulators—to its goals and to the way it does business. Therefore, it needs a fair level of narcissism to confront these challenges in a self-confident and effective way. Without narcissism, there can be no self-esteem.

Similarly, some debate and reasonable conflict about identity are good for preventing the organization from falling into the traps of unjustified narcissism. Some organizations, such as educational institutions, hospitals, charities, and churches, are continuously torn between social purpose and economic viability. The tension reflects the presence of conflicting identity anchors that, if not balanced effectively, can lead to confusion and, ultimately, organizational decline.

To conclude this review of identity dysfunctions, it is important for managers to recognize that, like individuals, organizations necessarily experience tensions in their identity. The healthy organization is not one that has a perfectly clear and accepted-by-all identity. Actually, such an organization may never exist. Rather, a healthy organization balances tensions in its identity. Although identity, unlike strategy, does not fall entirely within managerial jurisdiction, managers sensitive to the importance of identity can also make a difference in this area.

Endnotes

1. The *New York Times,* May 7, 1998: "Compaq Said to Plan Cuts in Digital Jobs."

2. Scott, A., and C. Christensen, 2005. "How You Can Benefit by Predicting Change." *Financial Executive*, 21(2):36–42.

3. By comparison, the Dutch Philips company transferred all small-appliance manufacturing to Asia in the early 1980s.

4. In forcing the company to face up to the new realities, Gerstner was greatly helped by the record losses endured by IBM under John Akers and the prospect of bankruptcy.

5. Ford Motor Company, *Annual Report,* 2000, pp. 4–5.

6. Ford Motor Company, *Annual Report,* 2001, p. 4.

7. *Le Figaro,* March 18, 2005.

8. Excerpt from an interview published in *Business Week*, March 14, 2002.

9. *Financial Times*, October 21, 2003: "Boeing Turns to the Benefits of Diplomacy: Career Diplomat Thomas Pickering Faces a Tough Task in Helping the US Giant to Change Its Culture."

10. *Crain's Chicago Business*, March 14, 2005: "A Chicago Jinx? Boeing's Bad Landing."

11. Andy Law left St. Luke's in March 2003, following disagreements with the managing directors of the London office about internationalization. However, the company's identity has remained, so far, anchored in the ownership structure and operating principles defined by Law and his colleagues at the time of its founding.

Casualties of the *I*Dimension*

What do Carly Fiorina, Jean-Marie Messier, Thomas Middelhoff, and Philip Purcell have in common? All four, two from the United States and two from Europe, had outstanding credentials as business leaders. All four were highly visible and widely acclaimed in their roles as chief executive officer (CEO). The firms they led were seriously challenged in the business and technological environment of the 1990s. Each articulated compelling strategic visions for their firms, and their strategies were initially hailed as sound, bold, and necessary. All four, however, lost their jobs in astonishingly public fashion. All four failed to deliver, in one way or another, the change they promised.

They had something else in common as well. They were all casualties of the *I*Dimension,* of a failure to understand and appreciate the significance of their firm's identity. Each became entangled in, and overwhelmed by, identity issues they did not intend to trigger. Their efforts were perceived, internally and externally, as detrimental to the soul of their firms and were openly resisted. As a result, the four executives found themselves at odds with the organizations and people they were supposed to lead. As their change initiatives stalled and became, in all four cases, a matter of public controversy, the performance of their firms suffered and much of the shareholder value evaporated. Although the four leaders were abruptly removed from office by their boards of directors, their dismissals were seen in the press as logical and long-awaited. Their fate shows that when the heart and soul of a firm are put at risk in the eyes of key stakeholders, it is not enough for a CEO to articulate a strategic vision and align the organizational structure and systems. Success in these contexts requires another set of senses and skills—those in identifying, understanding, and managing a firm's identity. Without them, leaders can fall victim to the *I*Dimension.* With these skills, they can increase the odds of avoiding Fiorina's fate.

Carly Fiorina

On July 20, 1999, Louise Kehoe wrote in the *Financial Times*[1] that "Hewlett-Packard has chosen one of the top business-women in the U.S. and one of the most competitive individuals in the high-technology arena to become its chief executive." A few days later, *Business Week*[2] concurred:

Can Fiorina, a medieval-history and philosophy major, succeed at this storied engineering company? HP's search committee members say there isn't a better fit. The leaders—Ginn, Hackborn, and current CEO Lewis E. Platt—came by their decision after each one detailed 20 qualities they would like to see in the new CEO. Then they boiled it down to four essential criteria that played to Fiorina's strengths: the ability to conceptualize and communicate sweeping strategies, the operations savvy to deliver on quarterly financial goals, the power to bring urgency to an organization, and the management skills to drive a nascent Net vision throughout the company. Ginn says the committee looked at 300 potential candidates, four of whom "would have been excellent CEOs." Included in the finalists was Ann

Livermore, HP's enterprise computing chief. "But Carly was the best," says Ginn. "We see her being HP's CEO for a very long time."

On February 10, 2005, Scott Morrison wrote in the same newspaper that "Hewlett-Packard yesterday fired Carly Fiorina as chairman and chief executive, ending a tumultuous 5½-year tenure at the computer and printer maker," during which much of HP's market value was wiped out (see Figure 4.1) after a yearlong honeymoon with the financial markets.

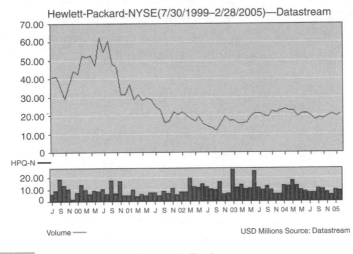

Figure 4.1 HP stock price under Carly Fiorina

How can a top executive, who dominated *Fortune* magazine's ranking of "The Most Powerful Women in Business"[3] for several years in a row, fail and be fired in such a public and humiliating fashion?

The majority of commentators were quick to explain Fiorina's demise in terms of strategic[4] and operating shortcomings; few[5] paid attention to the much deeper psychological dimension of the story. In many ways, Fiorina was at odds with the self-concept of the company she was brought in to lead. Even Fiorina's compensation package[6] appeared to be at odds with the founders' more egalitarian philosophy. By handing a technology company to an outsider who had proven marketing savvy but little background in technology, the board of directors took a big risk. Fiorina's integration was bound to be difficult in a company that had been managed for four decades by its founders (1938–1978) and then by two chief executives (John Young, 1978–1992; Lew Platt, 1992–1999) who grew up under the founders and who shared their engineering background and their commitment to the famed HP Way.

During her tenure, Fiorina took several initiatives that further alienated HP employees and were perceived, internally and externally, as undermining the soul of HP. In the first months of her tenure, for example, Fiorina launched a TV advertising campaign where she appeared in front of the Palo Alto garage where the cofounders started HP. Although her intent was to reaffirm the company's innovation heritage, Fiorina's central role in the commercial was received, internally, as a self-serving use of the founders' legacy. The decision to take the founders' last names out of the company's logo and retain only their initials sent another signal that Fiorina was de-emphasizing the company's roots.

The highly controversial and troubled merger with Compaq was another blow to the self-concept of HP. The merger threw HP into a business arena[7] that went against the firm's consistent commitment to differentiation through technological innovation. Although Fiorina won the proxy fight against Walter Hewlett, she paid a high psychological price for the legal victory. During the battle, Walter Hewlett was considered by many insiders as the legitimate and heroic representative of the HP Way, fighting against an alien mercenary. The announcement of 15,000 layoffs following the merger violated the sacrosanct principle of lifetime employment, another key anchor of the HP Way.

Walter Hewlett's sale of most of the shares owned by his father's estate and the voluntary or forced departures of about 20 key executives among former HP employees[8] widened the divide between Fiorina and the organization she had been chosen to lead. With her internal legitimacy seriously weakened and HP's business performance deteriorating rapidly, Fiorina's leadership was increasingly questioned, and ultimately she was fired.

The HP-Fiorina story illustrates how a company's deeply established sense of self can derail efforts to introduce far-reaching strategic and organizational change, and in the process trip up even the most seasoned executive. Ironically, Fiorina apparently read David Packard's *The HP Way: How Bill Hewlett and I Built Our Company* four times.[9] Despite repeated, and probably sincere, public statements about her respect for the HP Way, however, she seems to have failed to connect, personally and emotionally, with what made HP unique among all other technology companies.

Are we suggesting that Fiorina should have bowed slavishly to the HP Way and given up the rejuvenation mission for which she was recruited? Certainly not. But we are suggesting that had she been more fully aware of the significance of the *I*Dimension,* she might have approached the mission differently. In Chapter 9, "Masters of the *I*Dimension*," you will see examples of other leaders, operating in situations similar to those Fiorina faced, managing effectively with the *I*Dimension* and producing impressive results.

Jean-Marie Messier

In 1996, the French Compagnie Générale des Eaux (CGE) was an intricate web of more than 2,100 subsidiaries employing 250,000 people worldwide in a wide range of sectors, including water distribution (its historical core business), waste collection, electricity production, urban transportation, education, health care, casinos, catering, telecommunications, and real estate.

The roots of CGE reach back to 1853, the year of its incorporation by a decree of Napoléon III. Soon after its incorporation, CGE secured long-term contracts to supply water to the cities of Lyon (1853), Nantes (1854), Paris (1860), and

Paris suburban communities (1869). The company went international in 1880 when it was awarded a contract by the city of Venice, followed by contracts in Constantinople, now known as Istanbul (1882), and Porto in Portugal (1883).

At the center of the CGE web in 1996 was Guy Dejouany, then 76 years old, who led the growth and diversification of the company he joined in 1950, and who became its eighth chairman and CEO in 1976. At the time of his accession to the top job, water supply provided 46 percent of the company's revenue, and the balance was generated mainly in construction (28 percent) and energy (12 percent). Dejouany leveraged the company's close ties with national and local politicians to secure long-term contracts in areas other than water supply: waste collection, school catering, funeral services, heating, and so forth. He consistently used the cash flows earned in municipal services to feed investments in television, advertising, publishing, and telecommunications, to cite but a few areas where he involved CGE.

After two decades of consistent growth and profitability, Dejouany found himself surrounded by hostile forces. He and key aides were put under investigation for allegations of active corruption of local politicians. The real estate subsidiary, at the time overseen by his presumed heir, was deep in the red and was being investigated by the stock market watchdog for fraudulent reporting. In 1995, the company reported a $723 million loss—its first loss since 1945. In the same fiscal year, the total debt topped $10.5 billion and amounted to 125 percent of shareholders' equity.

Against this backdrop, Jean-Marie Messier, who had been with the company for two years as chief operating officer, replaced an embattled Dejouany as CEO in June 1996. In the following months, Messier performed radical surgery in CGE's business portfolio and sought to fix the balance sheet. He envisioned a company that would be involved in two core businesses— utilities and telecommunications. He proceeded to divest noncore assets and used the proceeds to reduce the company's debt. Operationally, Messier designed a formal organizational structure with clear reporting and accountability lines. To fix the company's reputation and ensure that the old business practices were behind CGE, Messier hired a former deputy to the Paris DA[10] to craft and oversee the enforcement of an ethical code of conduct to guide employees' dealings with clients—mainly municipalities and suppliers.

The first phase of Messier's tenure was unanimously applauded in France and beyond. John Tagliabue of the *New York Times*[11] dedicated a lengthy article to Messier under the headline "New Wave Chief Brings Life to a Creaky Conglomerate" and considered "Mr. Messier a perfect example of the young...modern manager on the move in Europe." The stock market reflected and reinforced the general goodwill toward the young CEO (see Figure 4.2).

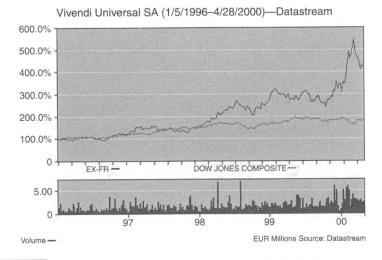

Figure 4.2 Vivendi's stock price in the first phase of Messier's tenure

The second phase of Messier's reign finished on a less heroic note. This phase began in 1998 with Messier's decision to change the company's name from CGE to Vivendi.[12] At that time, the dot-com bubble was swelling, and "old economy" businesses were suddenly out of fashion. Messier, whose company had stakes in TV, publishing, Internet access, and fixed and wireless telephony, envisioned a "vertically integrated global media and entertainment company." The name change was meant to signal a new era for the former CGE. To implement his vision, Messier disposed of other noncore assets and grouped and spun off all utilities businesses within the Vivendi Environnement subsidiary. The key stroke toward the new Vivendi came in June 2000 with the surprise three-way merger with Canal+ (the leading French pay-TV operator) and Seagram (then owner of Universal Studios and Universal Music). In Messier's own words, the resulting company, Vivendi Universal, "will be the world's preferred creator and provider of personalized information, entertainment and services to consumers anywhere, at any time, and across all distribution platforms and devices."[13]

Two years later, Vivendi announced $13 billion in losses, a historic record for a French company, and its market capitalization was down by 70 percent. The gap between its stock performance and the market kept widening following the announcement of the merger with Universal (see Figure 4.3).

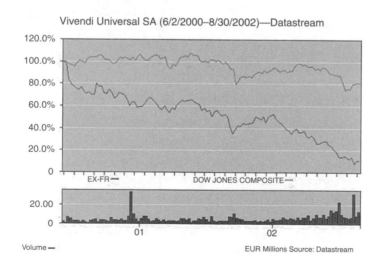

Figure 4.3 Vivendi's stock price in the second phase of Messier's tenure

After three months of hesitation, the board of directors pushed Messier out of the pilot seat. What went wrong?

Messier himself and many commentators blamed Vivendi's poor stock performance on the burst of the dot-com bubble and the severe punishment of Internet stocks. Other commentators saw the root cause in overpriced acquisitions that left Vivendi with a huge pile of debt and a mountain of goodwill on the balance sheet. Another opinion was that Messier put too much of his time into deal making, the activity in which he excelled previously at Lazard Frères, and neglected execution. Although there is certainly truth to all of these explanations, we believe that Messier was also a victim of identity issues he raised unwittingly and failed to cope with effectively.

In July 2001, a year after the initial announcement of the Vivendi-Seagram merger, and a few months after clearing the deal with regulatory agencies in Europe and the United States, Messier decided to move with his family to New York City and spend half of his time at the company's U.S. headquarters. The decision was interpreted in France as part of a plan to transform Vivendi into an American company. Bettina Rheims, the fashion photographer chosen by Messier to preside over the ceremony where he received the Legion d'Honneur, the highest distinction in the French Republic, expressed the reaction of the French intelligentsia:

When a Frenchman says, "I want to build an international company with the objective of cultural cross-fertilization," we can only be happy. But then the chauvinism that we have in each of us tells us to hope that this immense enterprise will also remain French and that its chairman will, with all the means at his disposal, help French artists to regain the place that they once occupied in the world and that they have, today, to a certain degree, lost."[14]

Messier did nothing to dispel fears that he might be American-izing a company whose history was so intimately associated with France and so much involved in French culture. He further complicated matters when he declared, in December 2001, at a joint press conference[15] with Barry Diller in New York, that "The Franco-French cultural exception is dead."[16] The statement was immediately relayed to the French media and elicited a string of angry reactions from politicians, intellectuals, artists, and employees. Gerard Chollet, a union representative, put it very clearly: "We don't like American imperialism, so when a Frenchman becomes the champion of that imperialism, we like it even less."[17] Fréderique Dumas, a film producer who made several movies for StudioCanal, a French subsidiary of Vivendi, said, "There's a feeling of betrayal. By moving to New York and appointing Americans to high positions within the company, Mr. Messier has turned Vivendi 'into a Trojan horse' against French culture."[18]

His initiatives alienated the French part of Vivendi, and Messier did not fare much better with his American audiences. American employees at Universal Studios feared the consequences of being owned and managed by a French company. On another level, the total divestment of the utility business, Vivendi Environnement, was part of the Seagram merger deal with the Bronfman family and was necessary to deliver the pure-play company that Messier promised U.S. investors. Unfortunately for him, the French establishment did not like the idea of a complete withdrawal from the utility sector. Jacques Chirac, then French president, was explicit about it:[19]

I am worried by what I hear about Vivendi Environnement. This company supplies water to a large number of communities and of French people. It is a vital company, a public service. One should be very careful that this company does not fall in wrong hands.

Messier found himself caught in the cross fire across the Atlantic about the soul of Vivendi. He did not realize that his personal and professional choices were loaded heavily with questions about his and his company's identity, and he was unable to come up with a satisfactory answer to the question about who Vivendi was. Ultimately, he and his company were seen as too French in the U.S. and as too American in France.

The Vivendi experience illustrates the danger of underestimating the significance of the *I*Dimension*. A firm's identity is anchored in the minds of both internal and external constituents, and a leader is insensitive to this at his or her own peril. It takes more than brilliant financial engineering, strategic prowess, and a name change to create one viable organization from many disparate parts. It requires skill in melding people from different backgrounds, sectors, and countries around a common under-standing of what the new entity is.

Thomas Middelhoff

July 2002 began with the demise of Jean-Marie Messier and ended with the fall of his friend and ally Thomas Middelhoff from the top of the German media conglomerate Bertelsmann AG. Reflecting on the rationale of Middelhoff's appointment to the top job at one of the largest and oldest companies in Germany, Matthew Karnitschnig and Neal Boudette wrote in *The Wall Street Journal*:[20]

Back in 1997, few people at Bertelsmann AG questioned the appointment of Thomas Middelhoff as chief executive. Then 44, Mr. Middelhoff had worked his way up through the ranks and seemed to embody the very essence of what the German media giant strived to be—forward-looking while firmly rooted in the company's proud traditions.

Reflecting on the reasons for the sudden termination of Middelhoff's employment on July 28, 2002, the *Financial Times*[21] wrote:

The company's controlling shareholders, led by the Mohn family and its patriarch Reinhard Mohn, and its secretive charitable foundation were said to have become increasingly disenchanted with Mr. Middelhoff's self-declared ambition to turn the German company into a media superpower straddling the Atlantic...The supervisory board and the Mohn family ran out of patience with a chief executive regarded, internally, as being increasingly out of step with the rest of his company.

To understand how Middelhoff got out of step with the company that he seemed to embody so well just four years before, one needs to understand something about Bertelsmann AG. The company was founded in the northern German town of Gütersloh in 1835 by the printer Carl Bertelsmann. Bertelsmann's first book was a compilation of Christian songs and hymns. He used his publishing program to support the religious Great Awakening movement of the Protestant communes in Minden-Ravensberg. He also published general education books and two newspapers. One of them, the *Evangelisches Monatsblatt für Westfalen* (*Protestant Monthly for Westphalia*), became the most important periodical of the Minden-Ravensberg Awakening movement and was published without interruption until 1929. From the beginning, community involvement was a matter of course for Carl Bertelsmann: He was active in the parish and municipal council in Gütersloh, he organized the communal welfare program, and he made a donation for the establishment of the Evangelisch-Stiftisches Gymnasium (local Protestant high school).[22]

Since its founding, Bertelsmann AG has been driven by the desire to reconcile business and Christian piety. Today, this philosophy is personified by Reinhard Mohn, the great-grandson of Carl Bertelsmann who led the revival of the company after World War II.[23] Over the years, the Bertelsmann family earned a reputation for its social conscience. In the late nineteenth century, the company became one of the first in Germany to offer corporate pension and disability funds. Later, Bertelsmann introduced paid vacation and other benefits.[24]

The private ownership and governance structure of the company reflect Carl Bertelsmann's belief that money must be considered a vehicle for generating social good. The Mohn family still owns 17.3 percent of the company, but the majority of shares (57 percent) are owned by Bertelsmann Stiftung, a charitable foundation. The voting rights of Bertelsmann Stiftung and the Mohn family (75 percent) are tied together and are exercised by Bertelsmann Verwaltungsgesellschaft (BVG).[25]

In his intent to transform Bertelsmann AG into a global media and Internet company, Middelhoff ran up against a number of deeply rooted beliefs and practices that constitute the essence of Bertelsmann. To realize synergies across businesses, Middelhoff sought to introduce centralization in a company where decentralization and entrepreneurship are sacred.[26] In a company where consensus is as deeply rooted as decentralization, Middelhoff alienated many when he announced publicly the sale of a profitable newspaper to raise funds for Internet-related acquisitions, without first discussing the proposal internally.[27]

In his effort to position Bertelsmann as a media and entertainment company, Middelhoff wanted to end the company's tradition of publishing educational materials and decided to sell Bertelsmann Springer Verlag, a publisher of academic journals and texts—regarded by the company as another meld of profits and good works. Although profitable, the company did not fit into Middelhoff's vision.[28]

While trying to make Bertelsmann into a global company, Middelhoff made public statements aimed at de-emphasizing the company's Germanness. His statements were echoed in the *New York Times*:[29] "Thomas Middelhoff, chairman of Bertelsmann A.G., the media conglomerate, would like to make one thing clear: Bertelsmann is no longer a German company. 'We are really the most global media company,' he says, with its

BMG music unit and Random House based in the United States."
In a similar vein, the *Australian Financial Review*[30] wrote:

Thomas Middelhoff says he is an American at heart. The 46-year-old
German chief executive and chairman of the nation's giant media
group, Bertelsmann AG, talks enthusiastically about things
American. "I love America," he says. "I describe myself as an
American with a German passport."

The full implementation of Middelhoff's vision of a global
media and entertainment company required, in his view, a new
ownership and governance structure for Bertelsmann AG. At
first the idea seemed acceptable to the Mohn family, but
Middelhoff was not allowed the time to implement it, and his
successor was quick to fold the initial public offering (IPO) plan.

Within four years, the combined effects of his strategic,
managerial, and symbolic initiatives estranged Middelhoff
from the company he was entrusted with and reinforced the
impression, internally and externally, that he was altering the
heart and soul of Bertelsmann. Middelhoff's abrupt removal from
the top job and his replacement by a less revolutionary CEO
shows again how difficult it is to introduce radical change when
such change goes against a deeply rooted identity.

Philip Purcell

The announcement, in 1997, of the merger of Morgan Stanley
and Dean Witter, Discover & Co. was greeted with mixed
reactions by analysts and commentators. According to the *Wall
Street Journal:*

Merging Morgan Stanley Group, a Wall Street investment-banking
firm with hundreds of corporate clients that want to sell securities,
with Dean Witter, Discover & Co., a brokerage firm with a
nationwide network of small investors, sounds logical enough. But

making it work is likely to be a task fraught with conflicts...Already Morgan Stanley's well-heeled investment bankers are fretting about how an alliance with a company that caters to mom-and-pop investors could tarnish their firm's 24-karat image.[31]

The turmoil in the management ranks in the years following the merger vindicated the skeptics and forced the departure, seven years later, of Philip Purcell, the man who, as chairman and CEO of a major publicly traded company, faced a revolt of virtually unprecedented public dimension in corporate America.

Most observers blamed the post-merger problems on a power contest between Purcell, chairman and CEO of Dean Witter before the merger, and John Mack, the former leader of Morgan Stanley. Other commentators emphasized cultural differences between white-shoe, blue-blooded investment bankers at Morgan Stanley and the salespeople on the Dean Witter side. A third perspective saw a possible source of the problems in the big gap between the pay scales of the two firms. Although each of these theories has its merits, we believe that the upheaval at the top of Morgan Stanley was due primarily to Philip Purcell's failure to sense and adequately deal with the perception among investment bankers that Morgan Stanley was losing its "elite boutique" identity and that the "Morgan Stanley" name was being hijacked by Dean Witter.

The seeds of the crisis were planted at the outset of the merger. Although the merger was actively pursued by John Mack and Richard Fisher, former CEO and chairman of Morgan Stanley, respectively, Purcell, former chairman and CEO of Dean Witter, Discover & Co., was given the top job in the new company. The decision was supposed to signal the parties' willingness to achieve a "merger of equals" and was, according to *The Wall Street Journal,* the first phase of an informal agreement that Purcell would step down in favor of John Mack five years later.[32] Meanwhile, John Mack would hold the President title and continue to oversee the investment banking business.

However, the "peaceful coexistence," as it was called by some insiders, between the two leaders began eroding as Purcell involved himself in managing the investment banking business and removed key executives reporting to Mack. With his room to maneuver shrinking, Mack threw in the towel in January 2001. His departure provoked the chain reaction that led, four years later, to Purcell's ouster and Mack's victorious return to the top of Morgan Stanley.

John Mack's resignation was followed by a severe talent drain in the ranks of veteran investment bankers. The management drain together with a poor stock price performance (see Figure 4.4) led a group of retired Morgan Stanley investment bankers ("The Eight Grumpy Old Men") to lobby hard with the board of directors to dismiss Purcell.

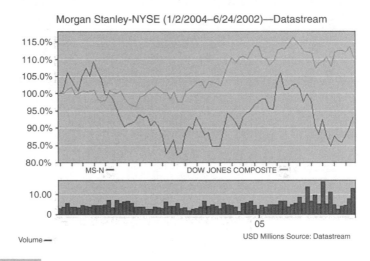

Figure 4.4 Morgan Stanley stock price under Philip Purcell

In response, the directors reaffirmed publicly their support for Purcell and asked the rebels for silence, but to no avail. The board eventually gave in to Purcell's opponents and accepted his resignation in June 2005. Moreover, despite initially stating that they had no intentions to do so, the directors rehired John Mack, thus, signaling the liberation of Morgan Stanley from Dean Witter and the restoration of its former identity. The climate of liberation was illustrated by the warm reception given by investment bankers to Mack upon his return to the Morgan Stanley headquarters and by the speed with which he removed former Dean Witter executives placed by Purcell in key investment banking jobs. Mack subsequently brought back several Morgan Stanley veterans who followed him to Credit Suisse First Boston (CSFB).[33] To further signal that Morgan Stanley had returned, Mack dumped the MWD[34] ticker symbol under which the company was traded in the stock market and replaced it with MS. Mack still has to show how he can improve the performance of, or prune, the business mix inherited from the merger,[35] but investors seemed to like the new Morgan Stanley, a mood that is reflected in improved stock performance (see Figure 4.5).

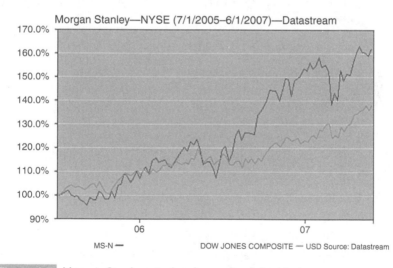

Figure 4.5 Morgan Stanley stock price under John Mack

This example illustrates what happens when the post-merger integration process does not reflect the interplay between the identities of the firms being merged. In this case, the identity of

Morgan Stanley was clearly more prestigious and attractive than the identity of Dean Witter, Discover & Co. However, the new management structure was dominated by Dean Witter and produced the impression of an outright takeover instead of the official "merger of equals." Had the architects of the deal been aware of the significance of the *I*Dimension,* they might have opted either for an organizational structure where each part would preserve its sense of self, or for the full integration of Dean Witter, Discover & Co. into Morgan Stanley under a Morgan Stanley–dominated management team.

Endnotes

1. *Financial Times,* July 20, 1999: "Prime Job for Outsider at Hewlett-Packard."

2. *Business Week,* August 2, 1999: "Carly Fiorina's Challenge Will Be to Propel Staid Hewlett-Packard into the Internet Age Without Sacrificing the Very Things That Have Made It Great."

3. Fiorina came up as number 1 in 1998, 1999, 2000, and 2001.

4. These strategic shortcomings included the failed merger with Compaq, continuing competitive pressures from Dell on the PC business, and difficulty matching IBM in enterprise solutions.

5. With the notable exception of Gary Rivlin and John Markoff of the *New York Times* in their piece "Tossing Out a Chief Executive" published in the February 14, 2005, issue.

6. According to sources cited by Rivlin and Markoff in the *New York Times* (February 14, 2005), the board granted her a $3 million signing bonus and a stock package worth $65 million and paid at least $2.25 million a year in salary and guaranteed bonuses. The board also agreed to pay the cost of shipping her 52-foot yacht from the East Coast to the San Francisco Bay Area.

7. This merger led HP into the commodity products arena, where competitive advantage depends on cost cutting, organizational streamlining, and layoffs.

8. *Fortune*, February 7, 2005: "Why Carly's Big Bet Is Failing."

9. This according to Peter Burrows, the author of "Backfire: Carly Fiorina's High-Stakes Battle for the Soul of Hewlett-Packard," who is cited by Rivlin and Markoff in the February 14, 2005, story in the *New York Times.*

10. "Procureur de Paris" in French.

11. The *New York Times,* October 14, 1997: "New Wave Chief Brings Life to a Creaky Conglomerate."

12. This initiative cost 60 million euros.

13. Presentation at Goldman Sachs, October 2001.

14. Johnson, J., and M. Orange, 2003. *The Man Who Tried to Buy the World.* London: Penguin Books, p. 9.

15. The press conference was held to announce the merger of USA Networks in Vivendi Universal and the appointment of Barry Diller as head of all Vivendi entertainment business in the United States.

16. The *New York Times,* December 24, 2005: "Remark by Vivendi Chief Unnerves French Film Industry."

17. The *Wall Street Journal,* January 4, 2002: "A French CEO's Taste for America Is Hard to Swallow Back Home—Move to New York Was Faux Pas for Vivendi's Mr. Messier."

18. Ibid.

19. *La Tribune,* May 24, 2002.

20. The *Wall Street Journal,* July 30, 2002: "History Lesson: Battle for the Soul of Bertelsmann Led to CEO Ouster."

21. *Financial Times,* July 29, 2002: "The American Dream That Ran into Reality."

22. Source: www.bertelsmann.com.

23. Bertelsmann AG was closed by the Nazis because of the devout Christianity of Heinrich Mohn, Reinhard's father. Its facilities were leveled by the British air raid over Gütersloh in 1945.

24. The *Wall Street Journal,* July 30, 2002: "History Lesson: Battle for the Soul of Bertelsmann Led to CEO Ouster."

25. Source: www.bertelsmann.com.

26. From the *Economist,* November 7, 1998: "Reinhard Mohn developed the doctrine after observing American business. The bosses of Bertelsmann's divisions have accordingly been encouraged to operate as independent entrepreneurs, with their eyes fixed on their own profitability, not that of the company as a whole."

27. The *Wall Street Journal,* July 30, 2002: "History Lesson: Battle for the Soul of Bertelsmann Led to CEO Ouster."

28. The *Wall Street Journal,* July 30, 2002: Ibid.

29. The *New York Times,* September 3, 2000: "Not Quite All-American, Bertelsmann Is Big on U.S."

30. The *Australian Financial Review,* May 8, 2000: "The Other Wunderkinder."

31. The *Wall Street Journal,* February 6, 1997: "The Morgan Stanley/Dean Witter Merger: Conflicts of Cultures Could Occur."

32. The informal agreement was mentioned by the *Wall Street Journal* of January 25, 2001, but neither Purcell nor Mack confirmed its existence.

33. *Financial Times,* January 7, 2006: "Mack Brings Back Morgan Stanley Veteran."

34. *Dow Jones International News,* January 11, 2006: "The New York investment banking giant has used the MWD symbol since Chicago-based Dean Witter acquired it in 1997. Veteran bankers have persisted in using MS as internal shorthand, and asked new Chief Executive Officer John Mack shortly after he arrived in July to change the ticker symbol, according to company insiders."

35. A common view among analysts is that the retail brokerage and credit card businesses inherited from the old Dean Witter, Discover are burdening the investment banking business and should be sold off. More in the *Financial Times,* January 17, 2006, story "Decision Time at Morgan Stanley—Staff and Outside Observers Alike Have Expressed Frustration as They Wait for Much-Needed Changes at the Bank."

To Blend or Not to Blend: Identity Integration in Mergers and Acquisitions

Two organizations are merging. Strategic synergies and cost savings have been identified, financial projections are optimistic, and the stock market has responded with enthusiasm. As the leader of the integration task force, your job is to make the merger work. You face two separate but related questions, both of which involve identity. First, do you want to blend the two organizational identities into one that a majority of people from both sides can identify with, or would you rather rely on minimum coordination mechanisms? Second, if you decide to blend, how do you do it effectively? These are two of the most challenging questions leaders face in the mergers and acquisitions (M&A) game. To address these questions, we first examine a case where they were not addressed effectively. We then introduce a framework you can use to weigh different models of identity integration and then choose the one that best fits the specifics of the situation you confront.

When the Sauce Curdles: The Case of DaimlerChrysler

As with a successful hollandaise sauce, a successful merger involves much more than the mere assembling of the necessary ingredients. The leader, like the chef, needs to have a deep understanding of how the ingredients fit together, of timing, and of the importance of regulating temperature. In the absence of such understanding, the sauce will curdle, as it did in the case of DaimlerChrysler.

After a decade of aggressive refocusing and global expansion of the former German Daimler-Benz conglomerate, renamed DaimlerChrysler in the aftermath of the acquisition of Chrysler in 1998, Jürgen Schrempp was forced out as CEO in July 2005. His departure provides another illustration of how even the most talented managers ignore the *I*Dimension* at their own peril.

The announcement of Schrempp's departure at the end of July 2005 inspired the following acerbic comment in the *Financial Times* Lex column:[1]

Mr. Schrempp will probably want to be remembered for creating a global group, dubbed "Welt AG." He is more likely to be associated with a long line of financial disasters: Chrysler, Mitsubishi Motors, Smart, Toll Collect. Even the Mercedes-Benz brand has been beset with quality problems.

The story of how one of the most admired European CEOs was suddenly removed by a supervisory board that ignored calls for action for several years begins in 1995. The former mechanic who joined Daimler-Benz in 1961 at age 16 was appointed to the top position. He undertook an ambitious expansion plan that sought to focus the conglomerate on making passenger cars and commercial vehicles. A statement taken from the company's Web site in 2002 explains how Schrempp wanted the recently merged DaimlerChrysler group to be perceived:

Our purpose is to be a global provider of automotive and transportation products and services, generating superior value for our customers, our employees and our shareholders.

To execute his vision, Schrempp paid $36 billion for the acquisition of Chrysler in 1998 and took credit for driving the largest industrial merger in history.[2] To add an Asian component to the envisioned global leader, in 1990 Schrempp further disbursed $2.1 billion for 34 percent of the troubled Japanese Mitsubishi and another $428 million for 10 percent of the Korean Daewoo Motors. Schrempp effectively rid Daimler-Benz of noncore businesses and focused the new DaimlerChrysler on vehicle manufacturing and related transportation services, such as the Toll Collection business. But he was less successful with the two other components of his vision: building a *global* and *profitable* powerhouse.

To build a global automotive company that could stand up to Toyota, General Motors, or German archrival Volkswagen, Schrempp completed only the first and easier half of the job— spending big money on acquisitions. He was unable to accomplish the second and more difficult half—integrating the quintessential German Mercedes-Benz with the iconic American Chrysler and the Japanese Mitsubishi.

To integrate the triad into a truly global company, Schrempp would have had to set up a truly global organizational structure and management team. Instead, and despite presenting the Chrysler deal as a "merger of equals," he pushed out former Chrysler top and senior managers and replaced them with German nationals. To compound the feeling of a German invasion of Chrysler, Schrempp said publicly that he deliberately used the "merger of equals" phrase to smooth the takeover negotiations but never really meant it.[3]

The indisputable Germanness of the new DaimlerChrysler group is captured in two key data points. First, while the company was still driven from Stuttgart by a 100 percent German management board under Schrempp's leadership, more than half of the company's global workforce was located outside of Germany. Second, on the revenue side, Germany accounted for one-fifth of the €124 billion (U.S. $169 billion) in total revenues generated in 2004, and the North American Free Trade Agreement (NAFTA) region generated €73.26 billion (U.S. $100 billion) compared to €47.39 billion (U.S. $64.5 billion) from Europe.[4]

How could Schrempp fully realize synergies across continents without an organization in which people from Chrysler, Mercedes Benz, and Mitsubishi could pull in the same direction instead of feeling colonized? Because he was so busy with "executive war room"[5] strategizing and had less apparent interest in the human side of the issues, he could not provide a satisfactory answer to this question. Instead of delivering the much-trumpeted value for shareholders, Schrempp actually shrank the value of the assets he was entrusted with. Under his stewardship, the combined value of DaimlerChrysler was less than the value of Daimler Benz before the merger.[6] The decision in May of 2007 to transfer majority ownership and control of Chrysler to Cerberus, a private equity firm, put an end to a process where smart strategizing and sophisticated financial engineering broke apart on the shoals of the *I*Dimension*.

Schrempp's inability to sense and cope adequately with identity issues stands in sharp contrast with Carlos Ghosn's quasi-obsessive message about the importance of identity matters in his approach to turning around Nissan and achieving synergies with Renault in select areas of purchasing and new product development. The contrast in stock price performance between the two companies (shown in Figure 5.1) is further confirmation

that Ghosn's approach, to be examined in more detail
in Chapter 9, "Masters of the *I*Dimension*," was more effective
than that of his German counterpart.

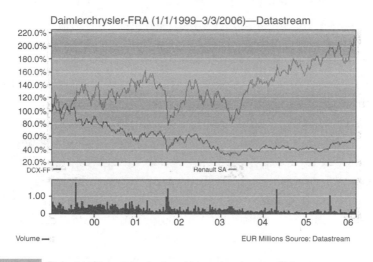

Daimlerchrysler-FRA (1/1/1999–3/3/2006)—Datastream

Figure 5.1 DaimlerChrysler stock price under Jurgen Schrempp compared
to Renault

What Path to Follow?

If managers can be seriously hurt in their M&A integration
efforts by failing to appreciate the significance of the
I*Dimension, what can they do to avoid this outcome? We
suggest that managers have a set of options for managing the
post-merger integration process. These options should be rooted
in an appreciation of the significance of identity issues. From
these options, managers can choose the path that best fits their
own circumstances. Addressing post-merger integration at the
level of identity requires that managers think through and
decide what to do with the legacies of merged organizations
(historical identities) and how to build a common identity for

the future. Specifically, managers should ask and seek answers to the following questions:

1. Can we or do we want to preserve the inherited identities of every merged organization, or do we need, or want, to delete some of these identities?

2. Do we pursue a common future through a new organizational identity, or should we integrate through inherited identities?

Table 5.1 combines the answers to these questions and results in four generic models of identity integration: confederate, federalist, symbiotic, and colonial. Each of these models corresponds to a particular treatment of the coexistence between the past and future of merged firms. We find examples of successful integration efforts in each of the four. This suggests that there really is no "one best way" when it comes to identity integration. It also raises questions about the value of claims made by consultants or highly successful executives that they have uncovered *the* secret of effective post-merger integration.

Table 5.1 Identity Integration Models

Building a common identity / Dealing with inherited identities	Through inherited identities	Through a new organizational identity
Preserving inherited identities	Confederate integration	Federalist integration
Deleting inherited identities	Colonial integration	Symbiotic integration

Colonial Integration

Colonial integration occurs when the identity of an acquired company is deliberately dissolved in the identity of the new parent. The process is typically swift. The acquired company is stripped of its name and visual identity (logo, letterhead, and so on) and adopts those of its new parent. The process sends a clear signal to the members of the acquired firm that they are expected to adjust and be loyal to their new employer. The dissolution of the acquired company also sends a clear signal to its external stakeholders (customers, suppliers, partners, unions, investors, bankers) that they will henceforth deal with a new organization.

Although the description of the process might sound brutal, it is not always or necessarily traumatizing for the members and other stakeholders of the acquired firm. The reactions of employees and other stakeholders depend on the depth of their psychological commitment to the dissolved identity, and on the perceived desirability and superiority of the identity of the new parent. To illustrate, when Microsoft buys a small technology company, its founders, employees, investors, and customers are most likely enticed to consider the acquisition as a positive event and will gladly trade the identity of a small, unknown company for the more desirable and prestigious identity of Microsoft. Because becoming a Microsoft employee is psychologically and, in all likelihood, economically rewarding for many people, members of the acquired organization have little incentive to mourn the defunct identity. General Electric has consistently implemented the colonial integration model. When GE buys a firm, anywhere around the globe, it strips that firm's identity and imprints its own on it. The process works in part because of the huge asymmetry between GE and its acquisitions. GE is more powerful, effective, and visible than any single firm it has acquired.

Colonial integration is less effective when there is not enough asymmetry between the buying firm and the acquired firm, or when the asymmetry plays out in favor of the latter. When the new parent and its acquisition target are comparable—be it in size, profitability, or reputation—members and stakeholders of the acquired company are tempted to feel that the identity of their firm is more valuable than that of the new parent. Rejection of the new parent's identity is further compounded when the parent is perceived as less effective, on some presumably important dimension, by the company it has bought. For example, the employees or customers of the target company may perceive the new parent as less innovative despite its large size. In other situations, the new parent may be perceived as a less caring employer or a less ethically driven organization. The perception that the new parent's identity is less attractive, or less valued socially, is often found in cross-border acquisitions. For example, European and Japanese companies have consistently had difficulty integrating their acquired subsidiaries in the United States, because U.S. managers tend not to think highly of the management skills and effectiveness of their European or Japanese "owners" and resent dissolution of their firm's identity into that of a foreign-based company.

Confederate Integration

Confederate integration is the opposite extreme of colonial integration. Here the merged organizations are allowed to preserve their historical identities and are not expected to meld into a new common identity. Coordination in this setting is kept at the minimum level necessary to achieve synergies in particular and limited areas.

The Renault/Nissan and, more recently, the Air France/KLM combinations are good illustrations of the confederate approach to integration. Instead of pursuing a full-fledged merger, which some might argue would have maximized expected synergies (on paper at the least) the management of Renault opted for a less intrusive approach toward Nissan. Renault sent a small team of French executives and experts to Japan to help Carlos Ghosn rescue Nissan. To achieve synergies quickly in the purchasing area, Renault and Nissan created a jointly owned purchasing organization incorporated in the Netherlands under Dutch law. To encourage new product managers and engineers at both Renault and Nissan to use common parts and platforms, ad hoc task forces were created. If the dramatic turnaround of Nissan and the record-high profits of Renault in 2004 are any indication, the approach followed by Louis Schweitzer, the former chairman and CEO of Renault, and Ghosn was highly successful.

The explicit reference to the Renault/Nissan design as a guide for the implementation of the Air France/KLM combination indicates that the "model" can inspire other managers. Although Air France formally acquired the Dutch airline in 2003, the deal explicitly specified that KLM would keep its brand name, its traffic rights, and its transportation certificate for eight years. Asked whether he would accelerate the integration of the two airlines, Jean-Cyril Spinetta, chairman and CEO of the Air France/KLM Group, explained:[7]

With KLM, we want to remain very pragmatic. Our group is made of two companies unified by a common share ownership and a tied economic performance and led by the Chairman and CEO of Air France....Our agenda thus is coordination....But in areas such as freight where branding is less important, we are ready to move toward more integration. (In the passenger market), things are more complicated....Rushed integration in this area could lead to disaster.

The Air France/KLM combination was met initially with hostility from French and Dutch employee unions, each side fearing job losses. The media was skeptical about the ability of Air France, an only partially privatized airline with a long history of losses and state subsidies, to succeed where Northwest Airlines[8] had failed. Two years later, the critics and skeptics were less vocal. Air France/KLM Group became profitable and was named the number one carrier worldwide[9] in an industry where many major airlines are struggling. Interestingly, Air France/KLM's stock has recently outperformed British Airways, the airline long considered the model to emulate for other European airlines (see Figure 5.2).

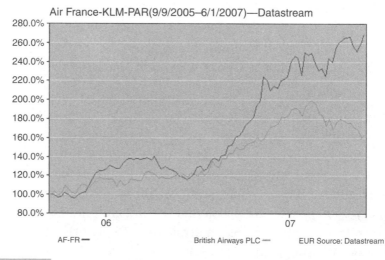

Air France-KLM-PAR(9/9/2005–6/1/2007)—Datastream

AF-FR —   British Airways PLC —   EUR Source: Datastream

 Figure 5.2 **Comparative stock performance of Air France-KLM and British Airways**

When should managers consider confederate integration? First, they should take a close look at desirable synergies and the ways to achieve them. Managers should consider confederate integration when a satisfactory level of synergies, on the revenue or cost side, can be achieved without tying the organizations closely together in day-to-day operations. In this case, broad strategic guidelines and a few coordination mechanisms are enough to ensure that the merged organizations pull in the same direction while maintaining their autonomy and identity.

The economic calculations should be supplemented by a serious consideration of the psychological distance between the merged organizations. Although it might have been optimal, in purely economic terms, to pursue more complete integration of Renault and Nissan to achieve more cost and revenue synergies, the fact is that the two organizations are very different. Although both make cars, the two firms have unique identities established through several decades and have grown in countries with very different cultures. Their people do not know one another, do not speak the same language, and deal with different suppliers and business partners. Furthermore, although Nissan was in deep trouble when Renault took over, the stakeholders of the Japanese firm were not prepared to let Nissan's identity be dissolved into that of a French automaker. In hindsight, Schweitzer and Ghosn's approach looks to have been the best trade-off possible between the benefits of tighter integration and the cost of ignoring the psychic distance between the two firms.

Although both organizations are European, the psychological and cultural divide between Air France and KLM is wide. Pursuing a confederate approach, carefully conveyed by the use of the French word "rapprochement" by the chief executives of both Renault and Air France, gives people on both sides time to get to know each other. Perhaps they can begin to forge a common identity on an informal, personal basis as well.

For the confederate model to work, people on both sides must understand how far the top management of the respective organizations is willing to go down the integration path. In the Renault/Nissan case, it was important that Renault managers, at all levels, refrained from adopting a "conqueror" attitude toward their Japanese counterparts when Nissan was struggling to recover from near death. Now that Nissan is thriving again, growing faster than Renault, and reconnecting with its glorious past, it will be equally important for Japanese managers to avoid arrogance toward their French counterparts. Much of the burden of maintaining mutual respect falls on the shoulders of senior managers on both sides. Recall the discussion of Morgan Stanley in Chapter 4, "Casualties of the *I*Dimension*." Much of the turmoil in the company reflected former Morgan Stanley key personnel's feeling that the identity of the investment banking side was being deleted by senior management from the Dean

Witter side. This was despite their commitment at the announcement of the merger to preserve the autonomy and distinctive identities of the two companies.

Federalist Integration

The key difference between federalist and confederate integration lies in preserving the identities of merged organizations while at the same time developing an umbrella, or overarching, identity, that each member organization can relate to, identify with, and thrive within. The image that comes closest to the federalist model is Russian nesting dolls, where each has its own existence and face and, at the same time, contains dolls with their own faces and beings.

The federalist approach seeks to develop a new layer of identity and identification on top of the existing layer. An example of federalist identity integration in the making on a large scale is offered by the European Union. Instead of asking, or expecting, the French, German, or Italian people to give up their national identity and adopt a European one, political leaders are shaping a European identity that can be laid over national identities. The federalist project will have succeeded, and is already successful to a significant extent, when the average citizen naturally thinks of him- or herself as "French and European" or "German and European," and so forth.

In business, federalist integration has been successfully and consistently implemented by Johnson & Johnson in the United States and the Paris-based luxury brands conglomerate LVMH. Johnson & Johnson is a household name and is recognized as a coherent global leader in the health-care industry. It operates through a family of 200 widely autonomous companies employing 115,600 people in 57 countries.[10] The management structure of Johnson & Johnson enables operating companies to have their own management structure and local identity. The integration of ALZA, the worldwide leader in drug delivery solutions, after its acquisition in June 2001 is a good illustration of the federalist approach at Johnson & Johnson. After the acquisition, ALZA retained its identity and managerial autonomy. Without knowing that ALZA is a member of the Johnson & Johnson family, one can hardly determine its relationship with Johnson & Johnson from browsing the subsidiary's Web site.

Bernard Arnault, current chairman and CEO of LVMH, has consistently reinforced the federalist model as a way to balance two contradictory imperatives. On the one hand, the federalist model preserves the identities of the unique organizations that feed and support LVMH's brands (Louis Vuitton, Moët Hennessy, Christian Dior, Kenzo, and so on). On the other hand, the LVMH corporate identity has enabled Arnault to put a recognizable face on a diverse portfolio of unique organizations and brands, thus enabling LVMH to achieve economies of scale and scope in selected areas: distribution channels, advertising, human resources management, and efficient access to financial markets.

Symbiotic Integration

Symbiotic integration is the process by which the identities of merged firms are dissolved and fused into a new identity that did not exist before the merger. The key benefit of symbiotic integration is the avoidance of uncertainties and anxieties among people on all sides about who are the winners and losers in a merger.

Efforts by top management to establish a new identity for the combined organizations create a neutral terrain. The process enables members on all sides of the merger to "forget" the identity of their original organization. This, in turn, smoothes the development of a common, shared identity, in which all parties feel they have equal voice and contribution.

Managers must ponder the benefits of symbiotic integration when the potential benefits of maximum strategic and operating integration are very high but the merged organizations have equally strong identities. In this setting, it is risky to dissolve one organization in the identity of another (colonial integration). Instead, managers should articulate a new, neutral identity where people and organizations with strong identities can build a common destiny and organizational framework.

In the pharmaceutical industry, symbiotic integration was illustrated by the merger of the French Rhone Poulenc with the German Hoechst. To preempt concerns about whether the French were taking over the Germans or vice versa, Jean René Fourtou, then head of Rhone Poulenc, and his German counterpart Jürgen Dormann, then head of Hoechst, decided to create a new, country-neutral identity. They gave the merged company a new name, Aventis, located its headquarters on the Franco-German border, adopted English as the working language, and made a concerted effort to assign the top 800 jobs in the new company on the strict basis of professional merit, not nationality.

SSL International, the result of a three-way merger between Seton (maker of Durex condoms), Dr. Scholl's (orthopedic footwear), and the London International Group (maker of disposable products used in hospitals), is another example of symbiotic integration. Instead of using the identity of one of the companies to integrate the others or keeping the merged companies at arm's length within a confederate or federal structure, Brian Buchan, a former Procter & Gamble (P&G) marketer, sought to create a new organizational identity for the merged company, a new identity that would replace the old ones. To build the new identity, he set up an integrated corporate strategy and organizational structure and picked a leadership team from the three merged companies. He also contracted with a business school, INSEAD, to design an executive training program where he, the leadership team, and about 200 key executives could get to know each other and reinforce the sense of belonging to the same organization.

The Four Models in Perspective

The four identity integration models offer alternative approaches to making one organization out of many. Each model represents particular trade-offs between how to deal with historical identities in building a common future. The cases used to illustrate each model show that all four can be successful when they are a good fit with the context and objectives of a merger and, more importantly, when they are implemented consistently.

From our observations of a large number of mergers and acquisitions, we can infer two common mistakes in post-merger integration. A first mistake is the frequent involuntary ignorance of identity in the formulation of a post-merger organizational design and management structure. Leaders who focus exclusively on strategic and operational alignment of merged companies cannot anticipate the implications of their decisions on the identities of the organizations involved in the merger. Leaders ignore identity at their own risk. And when identity is ignored, it almost inevitably comes back to haunt them and to jeopardize their carefully conceived, orderly integration plans.

Using language from one model and pursuing integration through a different one is another managerial mistake. Many CEOs, sincerely or cynically, use the symbiotic or federalist language to cover the reality of a takeover of the colonial type. By using the "mergers of equals" phrase, Jürgen Schrempp raised the expectation among Chrysler people of a federalist, if not symbiotic, design where the U.S. automaker could retain its autonomy, U.S.-born leadership, and identity. By admitting, two years later, that he had not revealed his true intentions, Schrempp confirmed an outright colonial approach that had become obvious.

Open admission of deceit is rare from a leader of Schrempp's caliber. But discrepancies between espoused and actual integration practices are a common fact of business life and fuel feelings among senior executives of acquired companies of having been lied to in order to secure their agreement to a merger.

To avoid sending conflicting signals, managers should keep in mind that contrary to strategic and operational alignment, identity alignment is not a "one-off" task but a process that can take several years. To ensure smooth identity integration, we advise managers to use the models outlined in this chapter in a dynamic way. This means that managers should be willing and able, under certain circumstances, to view identity integration as a gradual process. Again, the Renault/Nissan case will help us illustrate what we mean by gradual identity integration. Given the globalization of the car industry and the size of potential synergies and economies of scale, full-fledged integration of the two carmakers probably would have been the optimal solution. However, neither Nissan nor Renault was prepared for the colonial scenario (dissolution of Nissan in Renault) or the symbiotic scenario (full integration of the two carmakers into a new company). The large physical and psychic distance would not have allowed a federalist scenario, which would have meant the creation of a new identity and common management structure above the historical identities of Renault and Nissan. Therefore, the confederate model is probably as far as the two organizations were able to go as a practical matter at the initiation of the partnership, but it is clearly not the end of history. The next step will most likely be a move toward a federalist management structure where a central authority makes major decisions for the two carmakers (phasing of new product launches, more shared parts, more cross-assembly of cars, and so forth) while the two organizations keep their own management structures and operating autonomy. When the federalist phase has allowed for the creation of enough bonds and sense of common purpose, the time would be ripe for a full-fledged symbiotic integration, whereby Renault and Nissan would cease to exist as separate organizations and continue to be promoted as mere brands.

This hypothetical, though plausible, scenario is meant to show that leaders can gain from an understanding of identity integration as a long-term process and from choosing consciously among the four integration models to ensure viable and dynamic balance between theoretical synergies and organizational realities. Jean Cyril Spinetta,[11] the CEO of the Air France/KLM combination, illustrated this trade-off when he said:

Would we, nevertheless, move toward more integration? We don't rule it out upfront if it creates value. The future organization of the group will depend on value creation, not on a predefined scheme. We have created about ten task forces (cargo, passenger business, local branches, maintenance, IT, etc.) to investigate cooperation opportunities....To drive our alliance, we have created, for three years, a strategic management committee comprised of eight members, four from Air France and four from KLM, and where the Chairman of Air France has overriding voice. The system works well for now. We will see when the time comes if we should, or not, move toward a more classical organizational structure.

Endnotes

1. *Financial Times*, Lex Column, July 29, 2005.

2. *Business Week,* September 29, 2003: "Stalled: Was the Daimler–Chrysler Merger a Mistake? Many Say Yes—and Call for Schrempp's Head."

3. *Financial Times,* October 30, 2000: "The Schrempp Gambit—The Chairman of DaimlerChrysler Offers a Passionate Defence."

4. DaimlerChrysler company annual report, 2004.

5. The phrase was used by Schrempp in an interview with the *Financial Times,* October 30, 2000.

6. *Business Week,* September 29, 2003: "Stalled: Was the Daimler–Chrysler Merger a Mistake? Many Say Yes—and Call for Schrempp's Head."

7. *La Tribune,* March 22, 2005.

8. Before turning to Air France, KLM had been engaged in a strategic alliance with Northwest Airlines since 1993. The alliance proved a rough ride due to the deep divide between the American and Dutch airlines.

9. According to a company press release in November 2005, Air France KLM achieved the highest turnover in the airline industry (€19.08 billion in FY 2004–2005), had the highest market share among European carriers, and ranked third in passenger transportation worldwide.

10. Johnson & Johnson corporate Web site, March 10, 2006.

11. *La Tribune,* March 22, 2005.

When Should the Cord Be Cut? Managing Identity in Spin-Offs

In the March 7, 2005 issue of *Fortune*,[1] Shawn Tully wrote: "For investors who crave adventure, no area is more fraught with extremes of profit or doom than businesses newly liberated from the grip of corporate giants." The extremes Tully is referring to are illustrated by the contradictory findings of two reviews on spin-off performance. In 2002, the Booz Allen Hamilton consultancy studied 232 spin-offs undertaken during the 1990s by companies listed in the Standard & Poor's 500-stock index. In the two years following the split, the survey showed that only 26 percent of the spin-offs outperformed the index.[2] On the other hand, a more recent study of 88 spin-offs undertaken between 2000 and 2005[3] by Lehman Brothers strategist Chip Dickson found that spin-offs outperformed the S&P 500 by 45 percent, on average, in the first two years.

These contradictory findings suggest that spin-offs may succeed or fail in many ways and for a variety of reasons, and that no "one-size-fits-all" explanation is sufficient. If there is no "silver bullet," no single driver of spin-off performance, there may nevertheless be a way of understanding the roots of differential performance. Think about the impact of the *I*Dimension.* Spin-offs tend to be driven primarily by strategic and financial calculations. Add the more subtle, but important, impact of the *I*Dimension* to the calculus, and managers have a more sophisticated set of issues to take into account as spin-offs are planned and executed.

To illustrate, we use some well-known examples to demonstrate for managers the value of careful consideration of identity in spin-offs. We then put forward a set of recommendations for the effective management of the identity issues that spin-offs inevitably bring to the surface.

The *I*Dimension* in Spin-Offs

In studying a number of high-profile spin-offs, we found an interesting spectrum of identity outcomes. On one end of the spectrum, we found spun-off firms that continued to think of themselves, or to be perceived externally, by reference to their former parent long after the formal separation had occurred. On the other end, we found firms that were able to establish themselves as independent entities, with identities that were not linked to their former parent. Between the two were firms in ambiguous situations, free from their parents in some respects, yet still linked to them in the eyes of either insiders or outsiders. Table 6.1 shows four types of identity dynamics in spin-offs.

Table 6.1 How Identity Is Affected by a Spin-Off

Inside the spin-off / Outside the spin-off	Perception of discontinuity with former parent	Perception of continuity with former parent
Perception of discontinuity with former parent	Clean Break	Paradoxical Pattern (I)
Perception of continuity with former parent	Paradoxical Pattern (II)	Continuing Connection

Continuing Connection

General Motors established Delphi as an independent entity in 1999. A year later, Ford Motor Company followed suit and spun off Visteon. Interestingly, six to seven years after the fact, Delphi and Visteon continue to be closely associated with their former parents and to be defined as GM or Ford spin-offs.

Evidence of the difficulty Visteon has had in establishing itself as an entity that is independent of Ford comes from a variety of sources. Visteon's chief executive officer (CEO) and chief financial officer (CFO) held a conference with industry analysts at Lehman Brothers in New York in January 2006. The transcripts of the introductory remarks and ensuing Q/A session show that the name of Ford was mentioned 39 times, while that of Visteon came up only 24 times. Six years after the spin-off, Visteon is still tied to Ford by agreements regarding employment and pension liabilities. Ford is still Visteon's most important customer, accounting for 50 percent of Visteon's sales in 2005.[4] Further evidence of Visteon's continuing close ties with Ford is provided by the strong correlation between the prices of the companies' stocks (see Figure 6.1). This suggests that investors have not yet come to see Visteon as viable on its own and separate from its former parent.

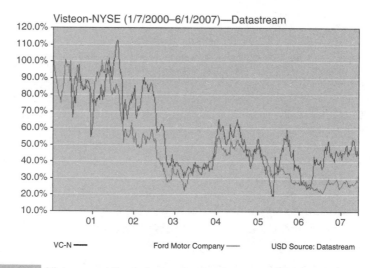

Figure 6.1 Visteon and Ford stock price performance (2000–2007)

Delphi's story parallels that of Visteon. In 2004, General Motors (GM) was still accounting for 55 percent of Delphi's sales.[5] Until the summer of 2005, the company was still driven by J.T. Battenberg III, a General Motors veteran who had led the spin-off. Although the new chairman and CEO, Robert S. Miller, has no employment history at GM, 20 of the 26 members of the leadership team (strategy board and corporate officers) come from GM. President and Chief Operating Officer (COO) Rodney O'Neal began his career at GM in 1971. Vice Chairman David B. Wohleen joined GM in 1978. Corporate officers with no employment history at GM hold functional responsibilities, such as accounting and general counsel.[6] As with Visteon and Ford, the close relationship between the stock prices of the two companies suggests that the investor community has continued to see Delphi and GM as closely linked (see Figure 6.2).

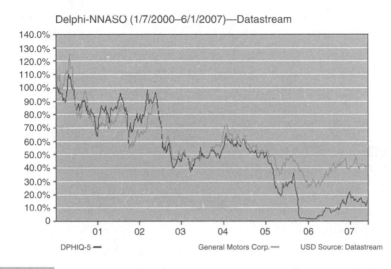

Delphi-NNASO (1/7/2000–6/1/2007)—Datastream

DPHIQ-5 ▬   General Motors Corp. ▬   USD Source: Datastream

Figure 6.2 Delphi stock price performance compared to General Motors

Although the management teams of Visteon and Delphi have tried to develop independent identities for their firms, other constituencies (analysts, journalists, investors, and employees) seem unable, or unwilling, to think of the companies independently of their former parent. Six or seven years after the fact, Delphi and Visteon continue to be defined as GM and Ford spin-offs.

Clean Breaks

Freescale Semiconductor is a good illustration of how a newly spun-off business can establish its own identity within a short time frame. Commenting on the 2004 spin-off from Motorola, Elizabeth Corcoran wrote in *Forbes:*[7] "Spun off from Motorola in 2004 amid much skepticism, (Freescale) is on the verge of moving beyond its former parent." Although Motorola is still an important customer, it accounts for only one-fifth of its former unit's sales. Further evidence of Freescale's success in establishing itself distinctly from its former parent is provided by the minimal reference to the former parent in the presentation of the company on the corporate Web site. Motorola is mentioned only as the former parent of Freescale, and later in the discussion of the company's products, Motorola is cited as one of the users of the chips made by Freescale. Michel Mayer, chairman and CEO of Freescale, has no employment history with Motorola. He was recruited to implement the spin-off and put together an executive team[8] with five out of twelve members, himself included, having no prior ties with Motorola. Out of the seven insiders, five had worked in the semiconductor division that was spun off. The comparative evolution of the two stock prices (see Figure 6.3) in 2006 is evidence that the investor community acknowledged the existence of Freescale as a separate entity whose fate was no longer tied to that of Motorola. Its merger on December 1, 2006 with an entity controlled by a consortium of private equity funds led by the Blackstone Group completed the break.

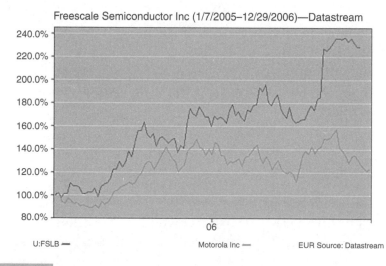

Figure 6.3 Freescale and Motorola stock price performance in 2006

The spin-off of Lucent Technologies from AT&T, in September 1995, is another example of a clean break between a parent firm and a business unit. That spin-off demonstrates how both parties can benefit from severing ties and thus clarifying their identities in the marketplace.

Reflecting on the spin-off, Bob Allen, then chairman and CEO of AT&T, explained:

The reasons for the breakup were several. First, there was the prospect of "dramatic change" in the communications industry. I concluded we all had to get more focused. Then, too, there was the trouble AT&T was having selling equipment to its competitors— particularly foreign telephone companies. It wasn't ever precisely clear that you lost an order, but it was clear that we weren't getting opportunities that we would otherwise have.[9]

By spinning off Lucent, and the computer business hosted by NCR, Bob Allen redefined AT&T as a telecommunications service company and allowed the equipment and computer units to establish themselves as self-contained entities in their respective environments. The move did not necessarily help AT&T establish a viable identity in the long run, but the spin-off was unanimously viewed as beneficial to Lucent and its stakeholders.

The following excerpt from a story by Catherine Arnst in *Business Week*[10] summarized well the challenges and opportunities facing Lucent at the time of the spin-off:

It could be a struggle for Lucent to remain No. 1. It will no longer have AT&T's guaranteed equipment purchases of about $2 billion a year. AT&T has promised to buy at least $3 billion worth of goods from Lucent—but only over the next three years, after which Lucent won't get preferential treatment. Lucent also must go through the wrenching process of cutting 22,000 jobs. And even though it keeps renowned Bell Laboratories, about 25% of the research facility's staff and resources will remain with AT&T....(However) Lucent has formidable advantages. It starts life with $19.7 billion in assets, including $448 million in cash. Also, with its connection to long-distance giant AT&T severed, it has brighter prospects for selling equipment to local phone companies. And it signed on a strong outsider as chairman—Henry B. Schacht, ex-CEO of Cummins Engine Co. and an AT&T board member. Richard A. McGinn, who ran the business since 1994, stays on as president.

The separate paths followed on the stock market by Lucent and AT&T (see Figure 6.4) reflect the recognition of Lucent, by customers, analysts, and investors, as an independent organization whose identity no longer needs to be defined by reference to its former parent. Although McGinn, the insider who played a prominent role in designing the spin-off, was expected to land the top job, the decision to place him, for more than a year, under Schacht's supervision helped Lucent establish its own identity. This view was well articulated by John J. Keller in the *Wall Street Journal*:[11]

(Schacht and McGinn) make an unlikely pair, coming from vastly different places but—so far, at least—proving to be uncannily complementary. Mr. Schacht, 61 years old, is an easygoing survivor of the Rust Belt of the 1980s who grew up with modest means but managed to attend Yale and Harvard. Mr. McGinn, an intense, ambitious 50-year-old, grew up middle-class in suburban New Jersey and attended tiny Grinnell College in Iowa before starting his career at Ma Bell. Together, they are tackling the huge challenges of imbuing the spinoff with a new identity and a more entrepreneurial culture....Shorn of AT&T's safety net and its name, Lucent has to overhaul a sagging effort in consumer telephones and expand sales of big network equipment overseas at a time when its proprietary technologies are threatened by hot-shot data-networkers and the vast Internet....Messrs. Schacht and McGinn also must convince multibillion-dollar customers—the Baby Bells—that Lucent has dumped all allegiance to their most threatening foe, AT&T....If the two men succeed, they will set a buoyant example in this era of restructurings: a spinoff that works.

Lucent struggled under McGinn, who was replaced by Patricia Russo. Russo was a well-respected executive who had left Lucent in 2001 to become CEO of Eastman Kodak, but who returned nine months later to take the top position. Under Russo, Lucent merged with French competitor Alcatel in 2006 to form a global telecommunications company, completing the clean break.

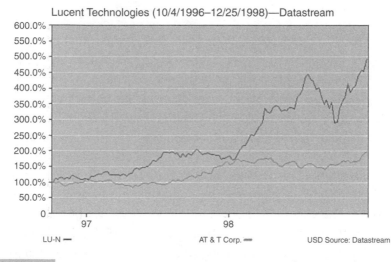

Figure 6.4 Lucent and AT&T stock price performance (1996–1998)

Paradoxical Patterns

In some cases, a close connection is maintained despite efforts to create a clean break. Consider the case of Agilent. It was spun off from HP in 1999 by Carly Fiorina in an effort to refocus the parent company on printers and PCs. In February 2002, less than three years after the spin-off took place, the following appeared in a story on the company in *Fortune* magazine:[12]

Agilent is run by three people, one of whom is alive. At the earthly level, there's CEO Ned Barnholt. Barnholt, a 35-year veteran of HP, sports big gold-framed glasses that droop slightly at the sides. He wears his gray hair in a comb-over. He is completely without pretense. When Barnholt, 58, chats with employees—something he does frequently enough that in the past six months he's given speeches to and taken questions from some 20,000 workers—they call him Ned; calling him "Mr. Barnholt" elicits giggles from employees. But while Barnholt manages the company, he seems to consider himself only a caretaker for HP founders Dave Packard and Bill Hewlett. All big decisions are vetted with the question, What would Dave and Bill do?

Indeed, the entire company functions on the premise that it is the real heir of Packard and Hewlett. When HP's house archivist had to choose between staying at HP or going with Barnholt, she went with Agilent. The company's Palo Alto headquarters is home to Hewlett and Packard's original 200A Audio Oscillator, which launched HP, and its labs still churn out testing and measurement devices. But even more, Agilent considers itself the true keeper of the HP Way— the management objectives devised by Hewlett and Packard that spelled out how to treat customers, shareholders, and most of all employees. The Way's key precept is that workers will give their best if they're treated honestly and listened to. In his 1995 book *The HP Way*, Packard asserted that making people feel that they are working toward a common purpose or solving a common problem creates "participatory management." To get there, all managers had to keep to a strict open-door policy and practice MBWA—management by walking around.

As of June 2006, eight of the top eleven executives at Agilent had spent at least 15 years with HP prior to the spin-off in 1999. The company is now moving aggressively to redefine itself as "the premier measurement company in the world," but, seven years after the formal separation from HP, it still seems to be closely connected to the former parent. How Agilent is Agilent? And how might the company have fared had the parental identity not been so deeply anchored in the former subunit through the mobility of executive talent from one to the other? Paradoxically, it would seem with the benefit of hindsight, Fiorina's efforts to redefine HP's identity through the merger with Compaq and the spinning off of Agilent did not serve the interests of either party terribly well, because the move created only ambiguity rather than clarity about identity for all concerned.

Accenture and Veolia illustrate another paradoxical pattern (type II) where insiders have a keen sense of being different from, and independent of, a former parent that outsiders continue to identify them with. To align external and internal identities, the management of the consulting business spun off from defunct Arthur Andersen replaced the *Andersen Consulting* name with *Accenture.* They also invested in a massive corporate branding campaign to ensure that outsiders perceived their firm independently from its former parent.

A similar process unfolded at the French company Veolia. It is now home to the historical businesses grown within Compagnie Générale des Eaux before Jean-Marie Messier renamed it *Vivendi* and set to redefine it as a global media and communications company. To pursue his vision, Messier spun off traditional businesses under the *Vivendi Environnement* name and put the new entity through an initial public offering (IPO) to generate cash for acquisitions in media and communications. Although insiders were able to see how much Vivendi Environnement differed from Vivendi, outsiders continued to associate them with each other. The identification became clearly dysfunctional when the former parent attracted lasting, worldwide, negative publicity. The decision to adopt a new name—*Veolia*—was meant to distance the company definitively from its former parent in the eyes of outsiders, and better align internal and external perceptions of its identity.

Why Spin Off?

The majority of spin-offs are driven by either financial calculations (unlocking shareholder value, dressing up balance sheets, or ridding a firm of troubled businesses) or strategic factors (trimming the business portfolio or improving its focus) or some combination of the two. The *I*Dimension* is rarely taken into account as spin-offs are contemplated. But what if it were? Might it not provide managers with an additional and potentially very useful set of factors to include in their decision-making process?

When might a spin-off make sense from an identity perspective? The first possibility is when the ability of a subunit to develop beneficial transactions with its environment is significantly hampered by being part of a larger corporate entity. The unit may have difficulty finding customers, attracting or retaining high-performing employees, being recognized and valued by financial experts, or simply benefiting from positive media coverage. Undertaking a spin-off in this context enables the unit to distance itself from its parent and engage with stakeholders who would otherwise pay little attention to it.

A second possibility is where nurturing one or several entities blurs the parent's identity and complicates the answer to the question of who the parent is. As discussed in Chapter 4, "Casualties of the *I*Dimension*," this was the case with Vivendi under Jean-Marie Messier. Messier clearly articulated his vision of transforming the former Compagnie Générale des Eaux into a global media and communications concern. But his failure to fully disengage the company from historical businesses alienated U.S. shareholders and the analysts who were expecting him to deliver a pure play.

When a spin-off is driven primarily by the identity needs of one or the other—subunit or parent—managers should expect the party that was forced to accept the spin-off to experience identity adjustment problems. When an important unit is granted independence to enable the development of a distinct identity, the spin-off may be perceived by internal or external constituencies of its former parent as an amputation of sorts. Managers who are aware of identity dynamics can help the former parent learn to think of itself without reference to its former unit and to adjust its own identity to the loss of an important component. According to several insiders, the decision to spin off the PC unit and swap its ownership for $1.25 billion and a minority stake in Lenovo triggered profound identity anxieties among many IBM employees. The employees took the split as a hit to their collective pride and, in the absence of a significant PC arm, have trouble continuing to think of IBM as an information technology (IT) leader.

Similar problems are to be expected when a unit is spun off principally to serve the needs or ambitions of its former parent. In this case, managers should expect employees, and possibly outside partners, to experience the spin-off as a sort of eviction or, worse, as a betrayal. Managers of the new entity must be prepared to help internal and external stakeholders feel positive about the split and to rally around a new definition of the entity without reference to its former parent. Altis Semiconductors, another IBM spin-off, illustrates this context well. Altis, a semiconductors unit headquartered outside Paris, was spun off in July 1999. Half of its shares were sold by IBM to Siemens. According to senior managers of Altis interviewed by the authors in the spring of 2003, Altis employees continued to think of themselves as IBMers and of the firm as an IBM entity.

The enduring tendency to define Altis by reference to IBM is clear in the following excerpt from a press release by the company on June 25, 2003, announcing the appointment of Elke Eckstein as CEO:

Altis Semiconductor, a joint venture between IBM Microelectronics Division and Infineon Technologies, was created in July 1999. Altis Semiconductor is located in Corbeil-Essonnes, France and employs directly 2,200 people. The company operates an SC technology campus hosting an additional 1,000 people from major SC industry.

Following her appointment, Eckstein, who had an extensive amount of experience managing joint ventures for Siemens, significantly changed the management team and sought to delete

IBM from the identity of the company, as can be seen in this revised definition of Altis:

Specialized in the manufacturing of state of the art electronic components, Altis Semiconductor is a major player on the semiconductor market in Europe. Located on a 55 hectare site south of Paris, Altis Semiconductor is at the cutting edge of technology, offering increasingly high performance services to its customers, world leaders in the New Economy.[13]

The third and final possibility where an identity-sensitive perspective might lead to consideration of a spin-off is when both parent and subunit could benefit from pursuing independent lives. In this context, the spun-off entity is free to realize its full potential under its own identity, and the former parent can better clarify its own. The spin-off of Medco by Merck belongs to this category. Merck acquired Medco in 1993 in the hopes of boosting its revenue and profits through owning a prescription management business. Ten years later, it became obvious that the expected synergies had not materialized and that the existence of Medco within Merck was a hindrance for both sides.

To prepare for the spin-off, Merck hired David B. Snow, Jr., an outsider, and named him chairman and CEO of Medco. Since then, Snow has profoundly remodeled the management team. As of April 17, 2006, of the 15 members of the executive board, six had joined Medco in the months preceding the spin-off or subsequently. Out of the eight insiders, only one had been employed by Merck before joining Medco. All other seven officers had been employed by the Medco division for a few years before the spin-off.

Since the split, Merck has encountered other, unforeseen problems that depressed its stock price significantly, but spinning off Medco has clearly enabled Merck to clarify its identity as a company specialized in drug research, manufacturing, and marketing. On the other hand, a born-again Medco was able to gain new business and enhance its profitability, and its stock price has nearly tripled since the spin-off (see Figure 6.5).

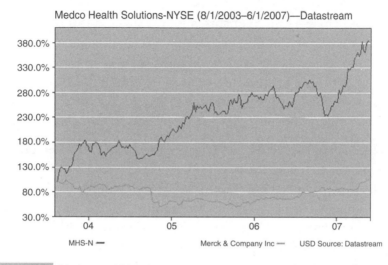

Figure 6.5   Medco and Merck stock price performance (2004–2007)

Managing the *I*Dimension* in Spin-Offs

When can a spin-off be considered successful? What can managers do to ensure success?

The easy and commonly accepted answer to the first question is that a spin-off is successful if it creates more value for shareholders. In assessing the wisdom and effectiveness of a spin-off, however, we should keep in mind the time dimension. Although it may be relatively easy to enhance shareholder value in the short term through a financially driven spin-off, we contend that sustainable value creation is possible only when a spun-off firm has established itself as viable and distinct, with its own identity. Framed with reference to the often-used DNA metaphor, this means that a spin-off is successful when it works well for both parties—when the spun-off entity has successfully acquired its own DNA and where the former parent's DNA has been successfully recombined to support life without the spun-off entity.

What can managers do to ensure spin-off success if they are sensitive to identity and its dynamics? To ensure smooth adjustment of identities, managers need to prepare the two organizations for life after the separation and ensure, through careful communication, that neither party to the spin-off feels that it is being punished or set up to lose in the process.

Second, managers should pay careful attention to the symbolic management of the spin-off. If they really mean to cut the umbilical cord, managers should be careful about how they name the new company and about branding issues. A name that contains or evokes the former parent does not help the spun-off organization establish itself as an independent entity, and neither does the continuing exploitation of the parent's brand in the marketplace. Even though naming and branding are important, as related by the discussion about Visteon, Delphi, and Agilent, bestowing a new name on the spun-off entity and inventing a new brand name for its product or services is not sufficient. However important these symbolic choices are, internally and externally, they alone cannot ensure successful identity adjustment. They need reinforcement with other, more substantive and consistent choices.

On the substantive level, special attention must be paid to the ownership, governance, and management structure of the spun-off firm. Again, when genuine separation is sought, the former parent should neither retain significant ownership in the spun-off firm nor keep a significant role in its governance. Given the significance of the top management team to the identity of an organization, a successful spin-off requires a new leader brought in from outside and a profoundly reshaped management team. This means that no matter how competent the incumbent management of the entity to be spun off is, bringing in outsiders will be required for the spin-off to succeed.

Finally, when managers are not under time pressure to perform a spin-off, traumatic consequences for both organizations can be significantly reduced if internal and external stakeholders are prepared for the spin-off several months before its actual implementation. In a successful spin-off, stakeholders on both sides come to see it as a natural and logical outcome. More importantly, they see the development of separate identities as a precondition for a healthy future for both.

Endnotes

1. *Fortune*, March 7, 2005: "How to Play the Spinoff Game."

2. Lucier, C., J. Dyer, and G. Adolph, 2002. "Breaking Up Is Hard to Do and to Manage." *Strategy+Business Review*, 28 (Third Quarter).

3. *Fortune*, March 7, 2005: "How to Play the Spinoff Game."

4. It is difficult to see how Mike Johnston, current chairman and CEO, will be able to bring the figure down to 14 percent in 2008, a target he announced at the Lehman Brothers conference.

5. Delphi Corporation, Annual Report, 2004.

6. From www.delphi.com.

7. *Forbes*, January 9, 2006: "Out of the Nest."

8. Michel Mayer was recruited from IBM, and he brought in senior executives from IBM and Dell.

9. *Barron's*, March 11, 1996: "Brave New AT&T."

10. *Business Week*, March 25, 1996: "How Glowing Is Lucent's Future? It Has to Face a Slowing Market—Without AT&T's Deep Pockets."

11. The *Wall Street Journal*, October 14, 1996: "Unlikely Team: An AT&T Outsider and a Veteran Join to Run New Spinoff."

12. *Fortune*, February 4, 2002: "How to Cut Pay, Lay Off 8,000 People, and Still Have Workers Who Love You. It's Easy: Just Follow the Agilent Way."

13. www.altissemiconductor.com/fr/index.php.

Identity in Strategic Alliances and Joint Ventures

Strategic alliances[1] have increased dramatically, in numbers and depth, as companies focus on core businesses, outsource peripheral activities, share investments and risks with other firms, enter new geographic markets, or venture into new sectors. However, the potential economic benefits of these arrangements often are not fully realized because of the complex set of factors that come into play when two firms attempt to work together. These factors include cultural misunderstandings, conflicting loyalties, hidden agendas, power games, and mistrust—all of which have been extensively discussed in the academic and popular management literature.[2] Not surprisingly, we believe that identity and identification issues play a significant role in the fate of strategic alliances, and that, if these issues are managed skillfully, they can help increase the odds of success.

Let us take a brief look at how mismanaging the *I*Dimension* can threaten the success of strategic alliances. First, when an alliance requires the creation of a new and separate organization, the venture usually draws its resources, including human talent, and competitive advantage from its parents. However, the more the joint venture is identified with its parents, the more difficult it will be for it to develop an identity of its own, internally and externally. The result can be pervasive ambiguity about identity, as the discussion of Airbus in the next section illustrates.

Alternatively, a joint venture may fail because the identity defined by its parents turns out to be an insurmountable liability. The case of Philips Consumer Communications, a short-lived alliance between Lucent Technologies and the Dutch Philips Electronics, illustrates how the initial identity of a joint venture can actually work against the realization of its potential.

Joint ventures can suffer from poorly defined identities or too-close identification with their parents. Even the parents may suffer if their identities are challenged by the success of the joint venture. Firms typically become involved in joint ventures to enhance their own strength in the marketplace, but highly successful joint ventures usually develop their own identities, internally and externally, and may ultimately seek independence from their parents. We illustrate this possibility in our discussion of Global One, an ill-fated strategic alliance between France Telecom, Deutsche Telecom, and Sprint. This venture failed precisely because the parents would not permit it to grow its own identity as a global provider of telecommunications solutions to large business customers.

Finally, alliances can raise identity issues by their mere existence, as demonstrated by the example of a Catholic hospital entering an alliance with a secular hospital. The Catholic hospital had to deal with the fact that its partner traditionally performed abortions, vasectomies, and tubal ligations. How then can the Catholic hospital reap benefits from this alliance while at the same time maintaining (not compromising) its core identity?

The first section of this chapter elaborates on the examples just introduced and shows how identity issues may emerge in strategic alliances and how these issues can jeopardize their sustainability and effectiveness. The second section lays out a conceptual guide for dealing with the *I*Dimension* in strategic alliances. There, we identify three questions that managers must ponder in the design of strategic alliances:

1. Is the alliance consistent with our identity?

2. Does the alliance require the creation of a joint venture?

3. How much do the partners want their own identities to be visible through the strategic alliance?

Consistent answers to these questions can help managers design sustainable and mutually beneficial strategic alliances. The final section proposes a set of practical recommendations for effective management of the *I*Dimension* in strategic alliances.

How Identity Issues Can Put Strategic Alliances at Risk

Managers who focus solely on economic calculations and neglect identity dynamics usually find themselves confronted by, and poorly prepared to deal with, issues they did not anticipate and that can severely impede the effectiveness of strategic alliances. The following discussion uses the four examples just cited to show how, in strategic alliances as in other areas, managers ignore the *I*Dimension* at their peril.

Airbus: An Industrial Giant with an Infant Identity

In July 1967, the French, German, and British governments announced plans to build a European aircraft with the long-term aim of challenging American domination in the aviation industry. A little more than three years later, in December 1970, a letter of intent from Air France agreeing to purchase six units of the A300 aircraft enabled the industrial launch of the program. In the same month:

The Airbus Industrie GIE (Groupement d'Interet Economique, or Grouping of Economic Interest under French law) is officially formed between Aerospatiale for France and a grouping of Germany's leading aircraft manufacturing firms, later part of Deutsche Aerospace. The Dutch firm VFW-Fokker and Hawker Siddeley of Britain is also associated with the programme. Airbus Industrie is to provide a single sales, marketing and support network for Airbus customers.[3]

Within three decades, Airbus grew rapidly and became a serious contender for global leadership in the aviation industry, but it was still a consortium with decision-making authority, facilities, and resources scattered across France, Germany, Spain, and the United Kingdom. If Airbus were to become a viable, economically efficient global leader, it needed to be organized as a single company—a move made by co-owners in January 2001:

The need to streamline the decision-making process, among other things, leads to Airbus reorganising itself into a fully integrated single company rather than a consortium. The European Aeronautic Defence and Space Company (EADS), a merger of the French, German and Spanish interests, accounts for 80 percent of shares while BAE SYSTEMS, the successor to British Aerospace, takes the other 20 percent. A Shareholders' Committee of seven members— five from EADS and two from BAE SYSTEMS—is set to approve major investments, budgets and new programmes.[4]

Although the move toward a unified formal organizational structure was an appropriate and necessary step, Airbus has yet to acquire an identity of its own and to exist independently from its parents. For now, when the name of Airbus is cited, it evokes immediately the European Aeronautic Defence and Space (EADS) parent group and its shareholders: Lagardère Group, DaimlerChrysler, and the French government. The close ties with its co-owners are simultaneously a boon and a curse for Airbus. On the upside, Airbus has been able to enjoy strong financial support from European governments to launch new programs and to secure orders from European airlines. On the downside, Airbus has not been able to establish itself as a stand-alone organization with its own management, decision-making authority, and strategic autonomy.

The difficulties posed by the reliance of Airbus on its parents are visible as the company is struggling to get the A380, its super jumbo challenger to the B-747, out of its assembly lines. Christian Streiff, the man who was hired in 2006 to pull Airbus out of severe turbulence, threw in the towel after spending three months in the pilot seat. Although he did not comment publicly on the reasons for his sudden departure, it is widely believed that Streiff tendered his resignation when he realized that he would not be able to act as the company's number-one pilot:

The 52-year-old former Saint-Gobain executive drew up a cost-cutting turnaround plan for Airbus that enjoyed strong support from EADS directors, but clashed repeatedly with the board over how the plan should be implemented and how much control he would personally exercise, according to officials familiar with discussions.

Mr. Streiff wanted to report to the parent company every quarter and have the final say on Airbus appointments, while senior EADS executives demanded closer oversight, said officials, who asked not to be named because the discussions were confidential.[5]

The decision to hand the management of Airbus to Louis Gallois, co-Chairman of EADS, does not enable Airbus to strengthen its own identity, and the company will continue to be seen as a high-potential venture still torn between its French and German parents. Can Airbus ever acquire its own identity? The answer will be positive only when its current parents allow it to fly on its own. This would very likely mean an initial public offering (IPO) and a new shareholding structure in which the current owners would agree to play a significantly reduced role in managing the firm.

Chapter 7: Identity in Strategic Alliances and Joint Ventures

Global One: A Short-lived Joint Venture Whose Parents Did Not Allow the Birth of an Autonomous Identity

In February 1996, the French France Telecom, the German Deutsche Telecom, and the American Sprint Corporation announced a three-way strategic alliance with the aim of challenging top-tier international carriers such as British Telecom and the then-thriving MCI. The French and German carriers invested a combined $3.7 billion to acquire 20 percent of Sprint Corporation (10 percent for each):

Each partner has handed over most of its international services and infrastructure to Global One to create a one-stop shop in a spirit of cooperation unheard of in the supercarrier market to date. "In many parts of the world, Sprint, France Telecom and Deutsche Telekom market and sell the same products and services to the same customers," said Deutsche Telekom chief executive Dr. Ron Sommer. "Now we have the chance to serve our customers through a single organisation."[6]

But how much of a single organization will Global One be able to be? In the first two years, the stars seemed aligned in favor of Global One, which was elected as the telecommunications alliance of the year by more than 730 users in 85 countries, who were asked to rate alliances on several criteria: "global reach, services offered, network quality, tariffs, service, and the number of responses a carrier received from outside its home market."[7] But soon after, Global One became synonymous with losses and public arguments among its founders: "Global One...has suffered from reluctance among the parent companies to hand over customers to the joint venture, and from disagreements over its strategy."[8]

Without effective transfer of customers and corresponding assets to the joint venture, Global One could not become autonomous from its parents and be perceived, internally and externally, as a full "being" with its own identity. The situation of Global One worsened after Deutsche Telecom launched a takeover bid of Telecom Italia in 1999. France Telecom launched a legal suit against its German partner on the grounds that the latter breached the strategic agreement signed between the two companies. In this highly charged context, Global One became the subject of a public paternity dispute between the French and German ex-allies, each circulating rumors that the other would eventually withdraw from the joint venture and let it take full control. The dispute created uncertainty about the true identity and final destiny of Global One:

Market watchers believe neither France Telecom nor Deutsche Telekom will choose to go it alone within Global One. The partnership is principally a repository for both companies' multinational business and both will be keen to keep those clients. The most likely option, therefore, is for Global One to be dissolved, leaving all three companies free to go after other partners.[9]

The prediction of imminent death for Global One was shared by many inside and outside the joint venture, thus prompting questions not about how Global One could survive the crisis, but about who, among the partners, would profit most from its dissolution:

According to Communications Week International, the Global One alliance...could be dissolved if the DT bid for Telecom Italia is successful. The report quoted a DT executive who said "Global One is dead. It will go under...soon. What we care about the most is that we get out of the alliance. All along it was never strong...never concrete."[10]

Further evidence of the difficulty in establishing a unique identity for Global One is the fact that it had three chief CEOs in its four-year life span.[11] After much controversy, France Telecom was able to buy out Sprint and Deutsche Telecom and to merge the entity into Equant, a newly acquired subsidiary.

The problems faced by Global One illustrate the costs of inconsistent identity management in strategic alliances. The three parents wanted the outside world, and particularly big customers, to see Global One as a one-stop provider of integrated telecommunications services. Internally, however, the parents did not want Global One to grow as a distinct entity having full control of its customer base and other assets. Had they been aware of the significance of the *I*Dimension* and anticipated the contradictory situation into which they put Global One, the leaders of France Telecom, Deutsche Telekom, and Sprint would have compelled the transfer of businesses and assets to the joint venture. This would have allowed it to build an identity of its own, or to define Global One principally as a coordination mechanism between the partners in some market segments and communicate this role accordingly.

Philips Consumer Communications: A Defensive Merger Cloaked as an Offensive Alliance

In June 1997, The Dutch firm Philips Electronics announced a $2.5 billion joint venture with Lucent Technologies, a U.S. firm:

The new company, Philips Consumer Communications, would be the world leader in corded and cordless phones and answering machines and is expected to generate an operating profit by the time the deal is finalised in October. Headquartered in New Jersey, it will have 12,400 employees and will also manufacture and sell digital and analog cellular phones, pagers and other mobile electronic devices. Philips will hold 60 percent of the joint venture and Lucent 40 percent.[12]

A little more than a year later, the management of Philips and Lucent announced the disbanding of the joint venture. There are undoubtedly several reasons for this outcome; we believe that the joint venture suffered from a poorly conceived identity. Viewed from an identity management perspective, the joint venture suffered from two problems from the outset—an inconsistent identity and a terribly hostile environment.

Although presented internally and externally as a joint venture, Philips Consumer Communications (PCC) was, in fact, a Philips entity. PCC was a business unit within Philips before the alliance with Lucent. Whether or not it was meant as such, the use of PCC as the name of the joint venture inevitably conveyed the sense that Philips was taking over the Lucent business against a minority ownership stake (40 percent). Colonial takeovers, whether real or perceived, typically provoke an "us versus them" divide. When the business is relatively stable and the environment relatively benign, these feelings do not necessarily put the firm's survival at risk. Managers can hope that, with time, people on both sides will get to know each other and will build a collective sense of "us." Unfortunately, the Philips–Lucent joint venture did not have this luxury. Philips Consumer Communications was born in a highly competitive and technologically volatile environment. To survive in such a context, an organization needs high levels of internal alignment and decision-making speed, two conditions that PCC could not meet:

Even at the time it was formed over a year ago few believed that the joint venture between the two companies, powerful as their joint resources and capabilities certainly are…could nonetheless catch up in a market moving at such a terrific pace.…The probability always was that a bicultural multinational organisation of this size put together from a position of weakness was always going to be too slow and lumbering to develop the rapid fire range of technically up to date and fashionably designed phone sets to accurately hit the early stages of overlapping and constantly shifting marketing windows of at best 6–9 months.[13]

As employees came under combined pressure from the marketplace and from parent firms' management, the level of panic in the joint venture escalated. The tendency on both sides to blame the other for failure escalated as well, as indicated by the following quote:

Philips complained that its partner had failed to develop the technology on time for a mobile phone with which it was to mount its challenge in North America. "We were sold a complete pup," a Philips official said.

Lucent...blamed frequent senior management changes at the venture...for a lack of focus that had led to "missed opportunities in mobile handsets." It is understood that the design of the special silicon chips has been changed four times in the past few months.[14]

Could the management teams of Lucent and Philips have done better? There is no easy answer to this question, because Philips was already suffering losses in this area, and Lucent was no better off. The two companies thought that combining two weak businesses would enable them to build a profitable leader within a year. Subsequent events showed that the respective weaknesses of the partners did not cancel out but, instead, compounded each other. In such a context, the birth and development of a new identity are problematic. In retrospect, it appears that the management teams of Lucent and Philips would have been better off either cleaning their respective houses before considering a possible joint venture or agreeing to a straightforward merger. This would have given full control to one of the two companies and preempted the temptation to place blame in the face of adverse circumstances. Had the management teams been sensitive to the significance of the *I*Dimension* as they planned for the venture, the outcome might have been different.

Riverside Health System and Mary Immaculate Hospital: An Attractive Alliance Stalled by Identity Anxieties

In 1998, the leaders of Mary Immaculate Hospital, which was founded by Roman Catholic nuns, and Riverside Health System, a secular organization, considered an alliance whereby the two Newport News, Virginia, health-care providers "would create a shared governing body, combine services and virtually eliminate competition between the city's two major hospitals....The proposed joint operating agreement is an effort to counter the growing power of Norfolk-based Sentara Health System, which owns Hampton General Hospital and 49 percent of Williamsburg Community Hospital."[15]

The economic and strategic benefits of the proposed alliance were obvious. But concern was raised among respective stakeholders about the identities of the two hospitals. Physicians and health-care professionals at Riverside Health System had traditionally performed abortions, vasectomies, and tubal ligations. These services were considered, internally and externally, as key to the hospital's mission. On the other hand, these same services were at odds with the deeply anchored identity of a Roman Catholic organization, as the following quote indicates:

Some doctors at Mary Immaculate have expressed concerns that they haven't yet been included in the talks. They also worry about what will happen to Mary Immaculate's nonprofit, Catholic character, and whether the end of competition between Riverside and Mary Immaculate would drive up insurance premiums.[16]

These concerns were mirrored at Riverside Health System:

Riverside is especially interested in continuing to perform tubal ligations, a procedure that blocks eggs from reaching the uterus. "Riverside has been a primary provider of that surgery, since Mary

Immaculate doesn't do them," said Dr. Barry Gross, a gynecologist and a member of Riverside's board of directors. "That's something we'd like to continue to provide."[17]

To accommodate both sides, Riverside management considered organizational solutions to keep the "problematic" birth control services out of the scope of the alliance. However, as the expiration of the six-month period of exclusive talks neared, the fears on both sides were not soothed. In a last-ditch effort to rescue the alliance, the leaders of the hospitals called on an outside consultant to provide a "neutral" assessment, but to no avail. The identity issues proved to be intractable. This example illustrates, one more time, the powerful influence of the *I*Dimension* on an organization's strategy. Had the leaders been sensitized to the perceived inconsistency between the identities of the two hospitals, they would have either discarded the idea of a strategic alliance or followed a more gradual, low-profile approach whereby the two hospitals would have been enabled to share noncore resources and operations without immediately triggering anxieties about their respective identities.

A Framework for Handling Identity in Strategic Alliances

The ill-fated examples just discussed show that managers can benefit from explicit consideration of the *I*Dimension* as they assess the rationale for, or design of, collaborative arrangements with other firms. Addressing the *I*Dimension* in the context of alliances means answering the following three questions:

1. How consistent or identity-threatening is a potential alliance for each partner?

If the odds for the alliance are perceived to be incompatible with the identities of one or more partners, managers should expect considerable psychological anxiety and resistance, internally and externally. If they still want to go ahead with the alliance, managers must know that calming inevitable identity-related anxieties requires time. This is more easily achieved through a gradual process of establishing bridges between people, helping them de-emphasize what they perceive as essential differences and emphasize elements that can bind them into a common destiny.

2. Does the potential alliance require the creation of a separate organization (with its own employees, resources, customers, suppliers, and so forth)?

3. How much of their own identities do the partners want to be visible in the alliance?

If the alliance requires a separate organization, managers can create a joint venture. They must be prepared to cope with the need for the new organization to develop a clear identity. This can be achieved by bestowing on the joint venture the identity of one of the parents (AOL Europe) or both (Fuji-Xerox), or by giving it an identity of its own (SFR).

If an alliance does not require the creation of a joint venture, the partners can opt for collaborative agreements or consortia and must decide how much of their own identities they want to be visible through the alliance. Here the range of options extends from giving the identities of all the partners a prominent role in the identity of the alliance (The Skyteam Alliance), letting the identity of only one partner be visible in the alliance (Bouygues Telecom), or de-emphasizing the identities of all partners in the alliance (EUCAR).

Table 7.1 summarizes identity design options in strategic alliances,[18] followed by a discussion of illustrative examples.

Table 7.1 A Framework for Managing Identity in Strategic Alliances

	All partners want outsiders to see their identities through the alliance	Some partners agree to keep their identities invisible or have little incentive to do otherwise	All partners agree to keep their identities un-noticed or have little incentive to do otherwise
The alliance requires the creation of a joint venture	1. The JV inherits its identity from both parents • Fuji-Xerox	2. The JV inherits its identity from one parent • AOL Europe	3. The JV grows its own identity • SFR
The alliance does not require the creation of a joint venture	4. Collaborative agreements designed to promote the identities of the partners • Sky Team Alliance	5. Collaborative agreements where only the lead partner's identity is visible • Bouygues Telecom	6. Low profile collaborative agreements • EUCAR

1. Joint ventures inheriting their identity from both parents: Fuji-Xerox

Fuji-Xerox is one of the oldest strategic alliances between an American company and a Japanese company. In 1962, Fuji Photo Film and Rank Xerox created Fuji-Xerox, in which each owned 50 percent of the shares. In 2006, Fuji Photo Film owned 75 percent of the joint venture. The sustainability of Fuji-Xerox has so far defied the standard prediction of instability, especially when the founding partners want their identities to be visible in the joint venture. How has Fuji-Xerox been insulated from the traditional conflicts between parents in a joint venture, especially when these bring together American and Asian partners?

Fuji-Xerox undoubtedly owes its longevity to a combination of factors; for present purposes, however, we will focus exclusively on the contribution of identity. Although the joint venture has carried the identities of both parents, Fuji Photo Film and Xerox have defined its geographic scope and management structure in a way that has enabled the joint venture to lead its own life independently from its parent organizations. Since its inception, Fuji-Xerox was given exclusive rights to the exploitation of the Xerox brand in the Asian region. Management-wise, Fuji-Xerox has always been a Japanese company driven by Japanese managers on behalf of the co-owners. In 2006, the Board of Directors included nine Japanese and three U.S. directors (including the chairman and CEO of Xerox Corporation), and all members of the executive team were Japanese. This design has allowed the joint venture to enjoy external recognition and market leadership through the Xerox part of its identity and to develop a consistent, fully Japanese, internal identity thanks to the preponderance of the Fuji side in the management of the joint venture.

Without a clear definition of the scope of the joint venture and a stable division of roles between parents, Fuji-Xerox would have been torn between competing claims for supremacy and would not have been able to establish and sustain itself for so long.

2. Joint ventures inheriting their identity from one parent: AOL Europe

In 1995, the German Bertelsmann invested a modest $50 million for 5 percent in AOL, and the two companies established AOL Europe as an equally co-owned joint venture. Five years later, Bertelsmann sold its 50 percent stake in AOL Europe to AOL Time Warner in a deal valued at as much as $8.5 billion.[19] During the five years of their cooperation, the external and internal identities of the joint venture were tightly aligned with its U.S. parent, while the German parent, a conglomerate involved in a variety of businesses, remained backstage. This asymmetrical division of roles between the parents allowed the organization to fully derive its identity from one and capitalize on the success and reputation of AOL worldwide. The arrangement was all the more interesting because AOL was still an emerging start-up at the time of the deal, and Bertelsmann was already a large, multinational conglomerate. Under such circumstances, the management of the more powerful parent is usually tempted to impose its identity on the joint venture instead of letting it assume the identity of the smaller parent. Again, the arrangement is viable as long as the shadow parent accepts its role in the joint venture and does not seek to come to the forefront.

3. Joint ventures with an identity of their own: SFR

SFR[20] is the second-largest provider of wireless tele-communications services in France and is currently co-owned by Vivendi-Universal and Vodafone. The operator was set up in 1987 as a subsidiary of the company then known as Compagnie Générale des Eaux (CGE).[21] Due to the financial and technological needs to develop SFR's Global System for Mobile (GSM) communications network in France, the management of CGE engaged in an alliance with Vodafone, which was able to increase its share in successive rounds up to the current 44 percent level.

Aided by the support of two powerful parents, SFR has been able to establish itself both as a brand and as an exclusively French organization. It has secured the number-two slot in the French wireless market and is a very profitable business.

4. Consortia promoting the identities of the partners: SkyTeam Alliance

Initiated in June 2000 by Air France, Delta Airlines, Korean Air, and AeroMexico, the SkyTeam alliance was subsequently joined by Aeroflot, Alitalia, Continental Airlines, CSA (the Czech airline), KLM, and Northwest Airlines.

The sustainability of SkyTeam and its competitors, One World and Star Alliance, owes much to the clear prominence of the identities of member airlines in the respective alliances. The three consortia were built to enable their members to better cope with the globalization of the airline industry and, at the same time, preserve their identities as independent organizations and brands. All three consortia are mere coordination mechanisms; none employs substantial staff or promotes autonomous products or services on the marketplace. Their identities are defined by and dependent on their membership.

The organizational form exemplified by the SkyTeam alliance is advisable when managers seek the benefits of close cooperation with other firms but do not want to run the risk of losing their firm's identity in the collaborative process. The formula is viable as long as those in charge of coordinating the alliance have a clear understanding of members' double agenda. Problems usually arise as some individuals or teams in coordination positions engage, consciously or not, in courses of action that are not mandated or sanctioned by all members of the alliance. These initiatives usually create tensions in alliances, because some members perceive them as contributing to the gestation of an autonomous identity that may eventually threaten, swallow, or at least overshadow their identities.

Are these organizational arrangements always good? The answer is sometimes "no," as in a competitive environment where the creation of consortia only serves to buy time for incumbent firms as independent entities, and delay market consolidation through out-and-out mergers and acquisitions.

5. Collaborations where the identity of only one partner is visible: Bouygues Telecom

In 2002, Bouygues Telecom (BT), the third wireless telephone operator in France by market share and birth date, unveiled a decisive strategic alliance with the Japanese NTT DoCoMo. BT was allowed to market the i-mode to its subscribers as of November 2005.

The alliance with NTT DoCoMo has been crucial in BT's competitiveness in the French marketplace. But the deal has no equity component, and the Japanese partner's identity is nowhere to be seen in the external communications of the French operator. One would have to carefully read the fine print in the company's communications materials to learn that i-mode, the cornerstone of BT's marketing strategy, is in fact the property of a Japanese company.

Is NTT DoCoMo getting the short end of the stick in this arrangement? Given the importance of the i-mode in BT's commercial and financial success, one would be tempted to answer "yes." One also might think that NTT DoCoMo should have secured an agreement giving it more visibility in the identity of the French operator and a significant ownership position. This line of thinking would be relevant if the managers of NTT DoCoMo had in mind an autonomous expansion strategy in Europe. The decision to promote the i-mode on the European continent through licensing contracts with local operators relieves the management of NTT DoCoMo from the burdens of bidding for local licenses, building subsidiaries, and promoting their identity. As long as NTT DoCoMo is satisfied with the current risk-return equation in Europe, the invisibility of its identity is not a problem.

6. Consortia where the identities of the partners are minimized: EUCAR

In identity terms, these organizational arrangements are the extreme opposite of global alliances among airlines. Here, none of the partners has an incentive for its identity to be seen through the alliance. EUCAR[22] is a good illustration of a low-profile alliance. Firms that are fiercely competing with each other in the marketplace join forces to share research and development (R&D) costs and lobbying efforts vis-à-vis European governments and the European Commission in Brussels.

Because it is mainly concerned with R&D, channeling public subsidies into private research, and "behind-the-scenes" lobbying work, EUCAR does not need to exist as an independent organization or as a brand. The less visible EUCAR is to the public, the less its members are viewed by the public as cooperating, and the more effective the alliance is.

The FIAT–PSA[23] alliance is a more-operational example of alliances in which members benefit from not giving the alliance an identity of its own and from keeping their own identity invisible in the alliance. Other automakers have followed the consolidation route to achieve economies of scale and global market presence, but PSA has consistently resisted calls to merge with or into other manufacturers. Instead, it opted for partnerships in different parts of the value chain. For example, when PSA needed an offer in the minivan segment, it joined efforts with Fiat to develop a product that is marketed, with slight variations, as the Peugeot 807, the Citroën CS, the Fiat Ulysse, and the Lancia Phedra. The two automakers have lasting and deep cooperation in minivans and utility vehicles, but their alliance remains invisible to outsiders and has not given birth to a distinct organization.

Managerial Implications

The foregoing discussion has shown that lack of sensitivity to the significance of the *I*Dimension* in strategic alliances can jeopardize their success. Also, there are several ways to manage the *I*Dimension* effectively. Managers can chose from a menu of options, keeping in mind that consistency and common understanding are key. When the partners in an alliance are keen on preserving their respective identities, they must be clear about it. They must promote the alliance through their own identities, as is the case in airline consortia, or give the alliance a low profile and leave their own identities backstage. On the other hand, when an alliance requires establishing a separate organization with its own resources and assets, the partners should be prepared to let it grow an identity of its own, give it the identity of one of the parents, or give it the identity of both parents. In the first case, the partners must be wise enough to keep their identities backstage and let the joint venture work toward establishing itself as an autonomous being in the eyes of its employees, customers, suppliers, and other constituencies. In the second scenario, the "silent" partner must accept that the joint venture derives its identity from and is identified with the other. In the third case, the partners must find a modus operandi whereby the joint venture can leverage the brand identities of its parents in the marketplace without creating confusion and tensions in the organizational identity of the joint venture.

Of particular importance is the understanding that a strategic alliance sometimes needs to establish its own identity to realize its potential in the marketplace. In this case, managers and employees of parent organizations must take a backseat and let the joint venture grow its own identity, internally and externally. Global One was a failure on this account, and it will be hard for Airbus to steal permanently the number-one slot from Boeing as long as its parents do not take steps to strengthen its own identity.

Another lesson seems to be that joint ventures cannot develop a viable identity and thrive if they are born under stressful conditions. When there is too much pressure on the people involved in a joint venture, the "us versus them" syndrome and the tendency to blame each other impede the development of a collective self-concept.

Finally, as a strategic alliance unfolds, the circumstances of the partners may evolve in ways that can make their collaboration problematic for one or both. When this occurs, it is important that the partners make the necessary adjustments. SFR is a good example for meditation. In recent years, Vodafone has been keen on integrating the company in its global organization, strategy, and brand, but Vivendi has consistently refused to cede control of one of the best cash-generating businesses in its portfolio. In the long run, the highly publicized legal fights[24] between the partners could be detrimental to SFR if the circumstances require further significant investments or if the business needs to expand out of France or into other business areas. As long as the status quo persists, it is very unlikely that Vodafone will ever allow SFR to grow out of France. On the other hand, as long as it does not have full control of SFR, Vodafone cannot integrate it into its global brand strategy. The same can be said for Vivendi, which cannot integrate SFR with its other assets in the telecommunications industry. These issues cannot be resolved without a clarification of whether SFR is a member of the Vodafone family, as the chairman and CEO of Vodafone likes to define it,[25] or a French mobile operator.

Endnotes

1. Although the terms "strategic alliances" and "joint ventures" are often used interchangeably, keep in mind that the two are not synonymous. Strategic alliances may or may not entail the creation of dedicated joint ventures. In this chapter, we use "strategic alliances" when we refer to interfirm collaborations in general, and "joint ventures" when we refer to collaborations entailing the creation of a distinct organizational entity.

2. For a review of the generic issues in strategic alliances, see Inkpen, A. 2001. "Strategic Alliances," *Blackwell Handbook of Strategic Management,* pp. 409–432.

3. www.airbus.com, Company Evolution, accessed December 13, 2006.

4. Ibid.

5. *The Advertiser,* October 11, 2006: "Chief Quits in New Crisis for Airbus."

6. *Australian Financial Review,* February 2, 1996: "Global One in the Big League."

7. *Exchange Telecommunications Newsletter,* April 17, 1998: "Global One Best Overall Alliance."

8. *Financial Times,* January 6, 2000: "Sprint Set to End European Alliance."

9. *Dow Jones Business News,* May 20, 1999: "Global One Venture in Doubt as France Telecom Sues Deutsche Telekom."

10. *Exchange Telecommunications Newsletter,* May 14, 1999: "Global One Survival in Doubt."

11. Viesturs Vucins (February 1995–February 1998), Gary Forsee (February 1998–July 1998), and Michel Huet (July 1998–January 2000).

12. *Reuters News,* June 17, 1997: "Philips, Lucent in $2.5 bln Phones Venture."

13. *The World Communications News Report,* October 25, 1998: "Philips and Lucent Abort Costly and Overambitious PCC Endeavour Losing $140m/qtr."

14. *Financial Times,* October 23, 1998: "Lucent and Philips Abandon Mobile Phone Joint Venture."

15. The *Virginian-Pilot,* May 28, 1998: "Newport News's Two Major Hospitals, Riverside Health System and Mary Immaculate Hospital, Outline a Joint Agreement That Would End Competition."

16. *Daily Press of Newport News,* August 8, 1998: "Hospital Considers Alliance."

17. The *Washington Times,* August 13, 1998: "Catholic Hospital in Difficult Alliance."

18. It goes without saying that factors other than identity can sometimes weigh in the structural design of alliances: regulatory constraints, respective market shares of the partners. Although managers can give more priority to some of these factors, they must be aware of their identity consequences and be prepared to deal with them effectively.

19. The *Wall Street Journal,* March 17, 2000: "Bertelsmann Set to Sell AOL Europe Shares to AOL."

20. The acronym for Société France de Radiotéléphonie.

21. The company was renamed Vivendi by Jean-Marie Messier in 1998.

22. The European Council for Automotive R&D.

23. Fiat, the Italian automaker, markets the Fiat and Lancia brands. PSA, the French automaker, markets the Peugeot and Citroën brands.

24. In 2002, the partners went to court to settle their dispute. Vivendi won and signed a four-year "nonaggression" pact with Vivendi. The pact expired in 2006, thus reopening the battle over the control of SFR.

25. *Dow Jones International News,* February 24, 2004: "Vodafone CEO: SFR Will Eventually Be Part of 'Family.'"

Managing the *I*Dimension* at Organizational and Brand Levels

If you are an average consumer with no particular interest in business strategies, you probably do not know that the RCA flat-screen TV you bought last weekend at the local Sears store is actually made by TCL Multimedia Technology Holdings. You are even less likely to be aware that TCL is a Chinese company that became the world's leading manufacturer of TVs, with 17.16 million produced in 2004,[1] ahead of the Korean giant Samsung. How much did you know or want to know about the firm behind the TV before buying it? Not much.

Now, assume that you also acquired a Harley-Davidson motorcycle. How much did you know about the organization that makes it? In all likelihood, you knew much more about "Harley-Davidson-the-organization" than you knew about TCL. How much did this knowledge matter in your decision to buy a Harley instead of a comparable Honda or Yamaha? It mattered a great deal. So the identity of the organization that made your bike was more visible and mattered a lot more to you than the identity of the firm that produced your TV set.

Now, let us ask how you can spend one or two thousand dollars on a TV without having a clue about the identity of its maker, but you pay much more attention to the identity of the firm that makes your motorcycle. When shopping for a TV, you probably looked at the brand and felt comfortable with the household name "RCA." A quick consideration of key technical and physical characteristics (appearance, screen size, bulkiness, picture and sound quality) and an equally quick and easy price comparison were enough to help you make a decision. Even if you wanted to know who makes RCA TV, the sales representative in the audio/video section would have most certainly been unable to tell you about TCL, because the Chinese company deliberately keeps its identity hidden behind the brands in its portfolio.[2] But when you bought the Harley, you knew and cared more about who made it because the management of Harley-Davidson deliberately puts the identity of the organization forward. It wants customers to feel that by acquiring a Harley, they are connecting with a special organization and a special social group.

This example suggests that as customers, we sometimes buy products without knowing, or caring to know, about the organizations behind them. At other times, we know and care a lot more about the identities of the organizations we buy from. When we consider the question from a managerial perspective, we see companies opting for two opposite strategies. Some organizations such as Harley-Davidson, Bang & Olufsen, The Body Shop, Ben & Jerry's, and Sony, deliberately want outsiders to see the connection between the brand and some unique attributes (identity) of the organization behind it. At the opposite extreme, companies such as Procter & Gamble, Unilever, LVMH, Altria, Nestlé, and TCL do not insist on showing the relationships between brands and the organization behind them.

To help managers make the right decisions about the relationships between brand and organizational identities, the next section discusses situations in which dysfunctional tight coupling between an organizational identity and a brand identity

actually destroyed a great deal of the brand's equity. Building
on the dysfunctional examples, this chapter then deals
with how managers can approach the relationship between
organizational and brand identities. Next, we introduce a
typology that sums up different configurations and that
provides managers a compass to guide them in a deliberate
strategy to help organizational and brand identities coexist.
Then we examine firms making the transition from exploiting
a single eponymous brand to developing a brand portfolio,
and we highlight the issues encountered in the process. Finally,
we build on the identity integration framework introduced in
Chapter 5, where we introduced the four models of identity
integration. We also propose guidelines to help managers deal
with the organization-brand theme in post-merger and
acquisition contexts.

When Tying a Brand's Identity to an Organization's Self-Concept Destroys Economic Value

Business history is full of examples of once-great brands that
were severely or definitively hurt by the inability of their
mother organization to reinvent itself. Recent examples of this
phenomenon are Polaroid and Moulinex, the defunct French
maker of small appliances.

The Polaroid and Moulinex brands were intimately tied to and
supported over several decades by organizations with unique,
strong organizational identities. However, the organizational
identities of Polaroid and Moulinex became huge liabilities
for their brands and almost destroyed them. Polaroid's inability
to distance itself from instant photography and Moulinex's
inability to escape its view of itself as a French industrial
company were responsible for the steady decline of sales and
profits despite the goodwill and strong recognition enjoyed by

their brands. Moulinex, for example, was elected as the "Brand of the Century" in 1997 by a panel of 5,694 French families and 11,438 individuals ages 15 and up. At the same time, Moulinex-the-firm was already on the brink of bankruptcy.

In both cases, the brands could be rescued only after the formal death of their parent organizations. Polaroid's demise is illustrated in Figure 8.1. As you can see, its price plummeted from a high of nearly $60 in mid-1997 to $0 in late 2001. The Polaroid brand was revived by a private equity fund, One Equity Partners, that bought a majority stake in the bankrupt Polaroid Corporation in 2002 for a mere $52 million. The investors liquidated the Polaroid Corporation—Polaroid-the-organization—after stripping off the Polaroid brand. They then created a new company in an attempt to breathe life into a Polaroid brand that was no longer as heavily tied to instant photography as it once was. Three years later, they sold the new Polaroid business to Petters, the U.S. consumer electronics group, for $426 million.[3] By liberating the brand from a mother organization with a dysfunctional identity, One Equity Partners was able to realize a handsome profit.

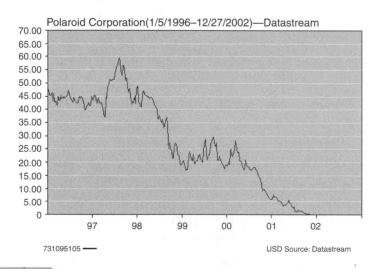

Figure 8.1 Polaroid stock price performance (1997–2003)

The story of Moulinex is similar. Despite several attempts by three successive management teams between 1986 and 2001 to save Moulinex-the-organization as a French industrial enterprise, the company was eventually put into liquidation. The brand now has a new lease on life within SEB, Moulinex's French archrival.

The cases of Moulinex and Polaroid show how once-valuable brand identities can be put at risk by being too closely tied to organizations that experience a downward identity spiral. The reverse scenario, although less frequent, is also possible. Organizations can also suffer from having their identity tied to a declining, controversial, or ineffective brand. Perrier is a good example of what happens when an organization draws much of its identity from a particular brand. In 1999, traces of benzene were found in bottles of Perrier sold in the United States. Source Perrier, the firm that owned the brand at that time, had to withdraw and destroy all stock of Perrier worldwide[4] and was forced off supermarket shelves for several weeks. The episode deeply wounded Source Perrier, the company founded in 1948 by Gustave Leven, who transformed the tiny mineral water spring in Vergèze, France, into a worldwide brand embodied by the famous green bottles shaped after "training weights." Unable to recover from the crisis, the company was acquired by the giant Swiss conglomerate Nestlé and integrated into its "Nestlé Waters" business unit. Because he did not foresee the possibility that the brand that drove the international growth of his organization could also drown it one day, Leven was forced to retire at the age of 78 on a "sour note"[5] a few months after the disaster.

We would not argue that Leven should have foreseen the events that brought down his company. Our point in using this example is to highlight the difference between brand identity and organizational identity and to show that problems with one can harm the other.

How Much Should Brand Identity Rely on Organization Identity, and Vice Versa?

The examples presented here illustrate another important facet of the *I*Dimension:* managers who are *I*Dimension*-sensitive think deeply about the right amount of coupling between an organization's identity and the identity of its brands. In weighing the options, they first need to know in which contexts customers care about the firm's identity as a whole, about the identity of its product brands, or both. When customers only see and care about brands, investing time and money on corporate branding efforts to promote the firm's identity can be pointless. Conversely, when customers need or want to know who stands behind a particular product brand, efforts to conceal the firm's identity may be counterproductive, especially when the firm's products may have negative health, ethical, or environmental connotations.

The majority of cases undoubtedly lie between the extreme situations of customers' total indifference or their high sensitivity to the firm's identity. TCL Multimedia Technology Holdings avoids being associated with RCA and Thomson TV sets because it is feared that customers might snub these brands if they realize a Chinese firm is behind them. The Turkish electronics firm Beko chose a similar approach with the iconic German brand Grundig. The steep decline of Grundig led to its takeover by Beko in 2004 in a $100 million deal.[6] Although Beko's management relocated all manufacturing operations to Turkey, they sought to downplay the new ownership of the Grundig brand. Eric Demircan, vice president of marketing, was clear about the motives underlying this approach:[7]

When we started the process of acquiring Grundig, we decided we had to manage the branding very delicately....We didn't want to emphasize the company that was acquiring Grundig as a Turkish company, because the brands have a flavor of the country they belong to. We didn't want to lose the feeling of Grundig being a German brand: solid, long life and a little bit conservative, maybe.

The cases of TCL and Beko illustrate contexts where too much association of a brand with a particular organization can lead to brand equity loss. In such a context, sharp separation between the firm's identity and the identity of its brands can be beneficial. The accidental fall of Source Perrier into the hands of Nestlé shows that close identification with a particular brand can be detrimental to the firm. Altria is another interesting example. Although it draws much of its profits from selling cigarettes, it does not want its name to appear behind Marlboro and other tobacco brands. By assuming a corporate identity that is independent from its brands and diversifying into the food industry through Kraft Foods, Altria is hedging against the risks entailed by operating in the highly controversial tobacco industry.

At the other extreme of the continuum, close association between organizational and brand identities is appropriate when it is clearly beneficial to one side of the relationship or the other. By emphasizing the Scandinavian roots and holistic philosophy of their company, the managers of Bang & Olufsen have successfully created a halo effect around the brand. The brand's good reputation, in turn, reflects positively on the organization in a sort of virtuous circle of growing sales and good profitability (see Figure 8.2). Similar approaches are observable at Ben & Jerry's before it was acquired by Unilever and by Apple computers. In all cases, the firm's identity is an important part of the value proposition to the customer. One of the challenges faced by Unilever was to avoid destroying Ben & Jerry's unique appeal as it was integrated into the company.

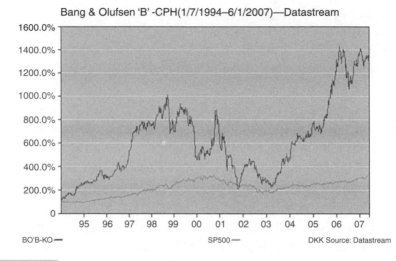

Bang & Olufsen 'B' -CPH(1/7/1994–6/1/2007)—Datastream

Figure 8.2 Bang & Olufsen stock price performance

The case of Danone illustrates how a company can benefit from identifying itself with a particular brand. The company has its roots in glass manufacturing and was known until June 1994 as BSN. This acronym came from the initials of three medium-sized French glassmakers merged by Antoine Riboud in the 1960s. When Riboud realized, in the 1970s, that his ambition to position BSN as a worldwide leader in glass manufacturing was likely to be frustrated, he undertook to divest the glass manufacturing businesses and made a series of acquisitions in the food sector. By the 1990s, BSN had become a de facto food company, but its identity was still associated with glass manufacturing. To signal that the company had completed its metamorphosis, Riboud decided to rename the company after its star brand, Danone. By naming itself after an internationally known and respected brand, Danone benefited instantly from the brand's reputation and recognition. The decision also meant that the firm had definitively turned the glass manufacturing page and was writing a new chapter in the food industry.

The name change following the acquisition of AT&T by SBC provides a more recent example of how an organization can attempt to benefit from the reputation of a brand that enjoys

98 percent name recognition among U.S. consumers[8] and is equally known worldwide. But differing from Danone, the AT&T name has been associated for too long with a declining organization unable to find its way in a deregulated and innovation-driven telecommunications industry. The decision to rename SBC after AT&T may make sense from an external identity management perspective, but it may be more problematic from an internal identity perspective. SBC employees may find it difficult to identify with a name that has become synonymous with corporate failure.

A similar issue is associated with the decision to use the US Airways name following the merger of that airline with America West. Although US Airways has greater national brand recognition than America West, as an organization it is associated with two decades of management missteps that seriously affected employee morale and ultimately pushed it into bankruptcy.

Assessing the Relationships Between Organizational and Brand Identities

The foregoing examples suggest that strict equivalence between an organization's identity and the identity of its brand can be beneficial for both under some circumstances but under others beneficial or harmful for either. The examples also suggest that there are situations in which careful separation between a brand and its carrying organization can be beneficial. What are the implications for management? To answer this question, we develop a matrix for diagnosing the relationships between organizational and brand identities. This matrix allows us to draw practical implications for managers who have to deal with problematic relationships between organizational and brand identities.

The diagnostic matrix is summarized in Table 8.1. The horizontal axis distinguishes contexts in which organizations and brands are either intimately tied or have distinct identities. The vertical axis indicates whether the relationship between organizational and brand identity is supportive of or detrimental to one side or the other.

Table 8.1 Diagnosing the Relationships Between Organizational and Brand Identities

	Dysfunctional relationships	Functional relationships
The identity of the organization and the identity of the brand are intimately tied	**1. Dysfunctional dependency** The brand is hurt by exclusive association with a declining organization or the organization may be hurt by too much dependence on a particular brand.	**2. The virtuous circle** The brand benefits from being associated with a unique organization and the organization benefits from connection with a unique brand.
The identity of the organization is distinct from the identities of the brands in its portfolio	**4. Absent or negative synergies** The organization does not add value to the brands or a diverse brand portfolio blurs the identity of the carrying organization.	**3. Brand equity protective separation** Brands have their own life and thrive without reference to the carrying organization

Cells 1 and 2 were extensively illustrated in the foregoing discussion and will not be revisited here. Cell 4 was partially introduced through the discussion of how the Turkish Beko and the Chinese TCL have deliberately refrained from associating their organizational identities with well-established brands in Europe and the United States. Procter & Gamble (P&G) illustrates another context in which organization-brand identity separation is beneficial to both sides. By enabling individual brands to have their own lives, the approach allows brand managers to focus on their customers and competitors and minimizes the time and energy spent on managing interfaces with other brands or dealing with corporate-level issues. The approach builds much of a brand's equity at the level of the brand itself and potentially enables P&G to add or subtract individual brands to and from its portfolio with no visible consequences for brand-loyal customers. While enabling its brands to promote their own identities in the eyes of their customers, P&G also managed to establish a unique corporate identity. The company is very well known as a leading consumer products company among suppliers, retailers, employees, investors, and business journalists. At the same time, it has invested so much in the promotion of its brands that very few consumers know that their favorite soap or diaper brand comes from P&G.

Even though Johnson & Johnson and LVMH, the French luxury group, provide other examples of the successful decoupling of corporate and brand-level identities, Unilever illustrates the limits of this approach and is a good example of what happens in cell 3. Until recently, the company owned up to 1,600 consumer brands, but the breadth and market leadership of its brands did not help it build a strong organizational identity. For decades, the identity of Unilever was trapped in its dual Anglo–Dutch roots. The dual identity was at the origin and reinforced a dual management structure that, in turn, did not allow the company to effectively support the growth of its brands. The lack of positive synergies between the brands and their carrying organization was reflected in slow growth and stagnating profits responsible for lackluster stock performance (see Figure 8.3), in comparison with P&G.

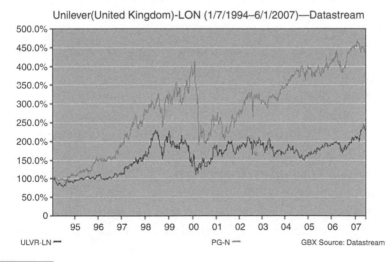

Figure 8.3 **A comparison of Unilever and P&G stock price performance (1994–2007)**

To reignite profitable growth, the former management of Unilever undertook radical surgery in the brand portfolio, trimming it to 400 from 1,600, and acquired such growth businesses as Ben & Jerry's, Slim Fast, and Bestfoods.[9] As shown in Figure 8.3, the stock market reacted positively to the program, but the positive impact on the stock price did not last long, leading analysts and commentators to ask for radical simplification of the management structure of Unilever.[10] This meant that Unilever had to do away with its dual identity and power structure. The long-awaited reform eventually came in February 2005 with the announcement of a single board of directors and a sole chief executive officer to preside over all Unilever businesses.[11]

Managing Identity in the Transition from a Single Brand to a Brand Portfolio

Industry consolidation, often driven by globalization, has led many corporations whose identity was historically tied to a single brand to acquire other companies and brands. In the car industry, Ford acquired the British Jaguar and Range Rover and the Swedish Volvo. Volkswagen acquired the Spanish Seat and the Czech Skoda. Daimler-Benz added Chrysler and Mitsubishi to its Mercedes star brand. In all three cases, the transition from single to multiple brands has proven a tough challenge for top management teams. To reap the benefits of consolidation and scale economies, managers are compelled to pursue maximum integration. This means dismantling acquired organizations and deleting their identities to enable full integration of the brands in the new parent company. In the marketplace, however, too much integration can pose serious problems for some brands. In this respect, Ford and Volkswagen illustrate two typical situations that managers confront. Although sharing platforms, parts, and production capacities across brands makes economic sense for Ford, Jaguar customers did not like the idea:

Ford discovered this when it based its X-Type small Jaguar on the Mondeo to save costs and speed development, prompting a furious backlash from buyers of large, expensive Jaguars. The X-Type, while less successful than hoped, has managed to bring in a new generation of drivers who could not afford one of the company's bigger cars. But it has also diluted the attractive exclusivity of the marque.[12]

The management of Volkswagen has to deal with another version of the problem. In this case, the detrimental effects of integration are felt by the historical brand, not by newly acquired ones. By stressing Seat and Skoda's membership in the Volkswagen (VW) group and giving them access to VW's state-of-the-art technologies, the company may be causing damage to its historical brand. Increasingly, customers are happy to buy a Skoda Octavia or a Seat Leon and save up to $6,800 on the price of their equivalent VW Passat or Golf models. Although integration in the VW organization has clearly added value to Seat and Skoda, this may have come at a high price for the VW brand. A similar issue faced the management of DaimlerChrysler as they sought to extend Mercedes' technologies to the Chrysler brand.

Ford and Volkswagen could learn from the way Toyota has successfully handled the development of Lexus. Although the cars are designed and manufactured by Toyota, the company's management has been able to give the Lexus brand an identity of its own in the marketplace and to differentiate it from both Toyota-the-organization and Toyota-the-brand. This has been possible due to an organizational structure that gives autonomy to the Lexus team while empowering it to benefit from Toyota's R&D advances and to tailor marketing policies to the brand's needs. To ensure that customers do not see a Lexus car as just an expensive Toyota, the brands have clearly differentiated products and features. Through this strategy, Toyota can give the Lexus customer a true luxury car that is not available for less under the Toyota brand name and the assurance, at the same time, that it is made by one of the best carmakers in the world. This approach has enabled Toyota-the-organization to use its identity as a launchpad for the new brand without interference from, or damage to, Toyota-the-brand. Toyota has used the same approach with the Scion, a brand designed to appeal to the youth segment.

Managing Organizational and Brand Identities After Mergers and Acquisitions

The preceding discussion raises two questions that follow any merger or acquisition: Should managers retain all the brands previously operated by the merged companies or drop some? And should managers preserve the identities of the merged organizations or delete some?

The answer to the first question depends on actual overlaps, or synergies, between the brands and on the ease with which a brand can be terminated or sold without losing the corresponding sales and profits. The answer to the second question takes us back to Chapter 5, where we discussed the four models of identity integration. Building on the identity integration framework, we suggest that managers consider two questions as they ponder the opportunity to preserve or delete organizational identities in the aftermath of a merger or acquisition. First, how much do the retained brands depend on unique organizations for their future growth? Second, what are the potential benefits of organizational integration after the merger? The implications of considering the two questions simultaneously are illustrated in Table 8.2.

Table 8.2 A Framework for Managing Brand and Organizational Identities in
Merger and Acquisition Contexts

	Potential gains from organizational integration are high	Potential gains from organizational integration are moderate
Brands have their own identities independent of any particular organization	Cell 1 Colonialist or symbiotic integration	Empty cell
The identities of brands are heavily dependent on the support of unique organizations	Cell 2 Federalist integration	Cell 3 Confederate integration

When potential gains from organizational integration are high
and the brands can thrive independent of the organizations
where they were located before the merger (cell 1), it is safe for
managers to consider full-fledged identity integration, of either
the colonial or symbiotic kind, depending on the balance of
power between merged organizations. For example, Volkswagen
was right to use the colonialist model in the integration of Seat
and Skoda, because the two acquired organizations were
relatively weak performers and could not support the
development of the brands.

When potential gains from organizational integration are high but
the brands need continued support from unique organizations,
as is the case for luxury brands, for example, the federalist
integration model offers a good compromise between the equally
necessary imperatives of coordination and autonomy of merged
organizations.

Finally, when the potential gains from organizational integration
are moderate, and the brands are dependent on the organizations
where they grew, as in the case of Renault/Nissan, confederate
integration is advised.

To conclude this discussion, we should emphasize that the
potential gains from organizational integration and the degree of

dependence of brands on unique organizational identities are a matter of managerial judgment. In the case of Renault and Nissan, for example, managers can be persuaded that the gains from tight organizational integration are potentially high. But they may deliberately refrain from pursuing them in order to give the organizations involved time to narrow the psychic distance between them before considering full-fledged integration of the organizations.

The decision by top management to use the UBS corporate identity and brand name for all businesses[13] across the globe suggests that coexistence between organizational and brand identities can evolve with time. After operating for years through a large number of acquired organizations and brands, management decided in 2002 that the time was ripe for integration under a single brand name. Mark Branson, chief communications officer, explained this to the *Financial Times:*[14] "The 1990s had been the decade of acquisition-led growth....Once the focus shifted to organic expansion, we had to pay much more attention to the brand."

Whether the deletion of acquired brands and the enforcement of the UBS brand name across all businesses and geographies were accompanied by a colonialist, symbiotic, or federalist integration model at the level of organizational identities is not easy to tell from the little we know about the internal processes.

The cases of Renault/Nissan and UBS suggest that individual brands can be considered heavily dependent on unique organizations. But in time, managers can deliberately work to weaken the dependence ties and prepare a brand to lead a new life within a different organizational shell or an organization to operate with a new brand. Similarly, the potential gains of organizational integration can be judged as low in the immediate aftermath of a merger but can be increased by managers through a first phase of systemic harmonization and psychological rapprochement of merged organizations.

Endnotes

1. TCL Multimedia Holdings company Web site, http://overseas.tcl.com/news/new.asp.

2. TCL's brand portfolio includes Thomson and Schneider TVs as well as Alcatel mobile phone sets.

3. *Financial Times,* January 10, 2005: "Petters Pays Dollars 426m to Acquire Polaroid."

4. *Financial Times,* February 15, 1990: "Perrier to Destroy World Stocks After Benzene Find."

5. *Financial Times,* June 30, 1990: "Perrier Founder Retires on Sour Note."

6. CNN.com, January 17, 2005: "Turkey Switches on to TV Market."

7. Ibid.

8. Company research reported in *Financial Times,* October 29, 2006: "SBC to Resurrect AT&T Name."

9. *Business Week,* August 6, 2001: "Unilever Restocks."

10. *Financial Times,* January 28, 2005: "Pressure Grows on Unilever to Ditch Twin Chiefs."

11. *Financial Times,* February 11, 2005: "Unilever Shake-up to Halt Slide: Anglo-Dutch Company Sidelines Co-chairman to Appoint First Sole Chief Executive."

12. *Financial Times,* September 23, 2004: "How Two Detroit Dreams Came Off the Road."

13. *Financial Times,* April 18, 2005: "Three Letters Gain a Personality: UBS, Europe's Biggest Bank, Has Collapsed Its Multiple Brands to Focus on a Single Global Name."

14. Ibid.

Masters of the *I*Dimension*

Although the firms they led, or are still leading, operate in different continents and different industries, the four leaders profiled in this chapter have three things in common. For starters, all four got the top job when their respective companies were coping with serious performance problems or even struggling for survival. Steve Jobs was called back to rescue Apple after the company had faltered badly under two previous CEOs. Peter Saunders took the reins at The Body Shop after the company experienced serious performance problems for several years. Louis Gerstner was brought in from outside after his predecessor nearly grounded IBM. Carlos Ghosn took the driver's seat at Nissan after Renault took control of a virtually bankrupt company. Second, the four have led remarkable turnarounds at their companies and have delivered impressive increases in shareholder value. Finally, all are masters of the ***I*Dimension.*** Each in his own way understood something fundamental about the soul of his company, and each leveraged this understanding effectively to achieve outstanding results. Steve Jobs *reconciled* Apple with its historic identity by reemphasizing innovation and design. Peter Saunders *leveraged* the unique identity of The Body Shop and used it as a platform for revitalizing the firm and repositioning its brand. Louis Gerstner *broadened* IBM's identity as an information technology company where mainframes, once synonymous with IBM, became just one part of a much deeper technology and solutions portfolio. Finally, Carlos Ghosn administered shock therapy to Nissan and sought, at the same time, to *preserve* its identity.

Steve Jobs

"Apple is becoming itself again." This statement, part of the title of a November 1998 *Fortune* magazine[1] story, captured the significance of Steve Jobs' return to the helm of the company he cofounded in 1976 and was forced to leave in July 1985. Five years earlier, the same magazine discussed the ouster of John Sculley, the man who pushed out Jobs, in a story titled "Odd Man Out."[2]

In the five years between Sculley's departure and Jobs' return, the company and its employees had a rough ride through successive crises. Apple's situation became so desperate that Michael Spindler, CEO from 1993 to 1996, vainly tried to sell the company to IBM, Sun Microsystems, and Philips, the Dutch Consumer Electronics group.[3] Gil Amelio, the man who led the turnaround at National Semiconductors, succeeded Spindler but could not stem the bleeding. Losses escalated from $816 million in 1996 to $1.045 billion in 1997; sales shrank dangerously from $12.72 billion in 1995 to $9.833 billion in 1996 to $7.081 billion in 1997 (see Figure 9.1). Under Spindler and Amelio, Apple's stock price continued to sink at a time when other technology companies were riding high on the crest of the Internet wave.

Spindler and Amelio were unable to cure Apple, but the seeds of its illness were planted under John Sculley. Although Sculley must be given credit for growing the company's sales from $983 million to $8 billion in the ten years of his tenure, he based the growth strategy primarily on traditional tactics of cost cutting and price competition—tactics that were at variance with the soul of Apple as seen by core employees and loyal customers, and more widely by industry experts and commentators. Furthermore, Apple's revenue growth in the last years of Sculley's tenure came at the expense of margins, and the gap between the firm's stock price and the market widened significantly (see Figure 9.2).

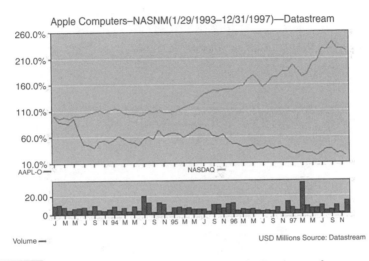

Figure 9.1 A comparison of Apple Computers' stock price performance with the Nasdaq index (1993–1997)

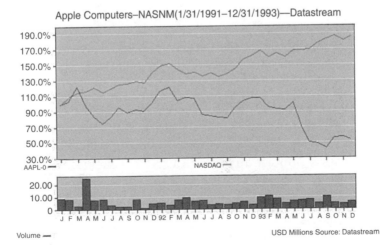

Figure 9.2 A comparison of Apple Computers' stock price performance with the Nasdaq index (1991–1993)

Fortune magazine's article "Odd Man Out" summarized well the general opinion, at the time, that Sculley's approach was at odds with the company he was managing.

Fast-forward to 2006. Apple's reputation for innovation has been revived, and the company is showing a net income of $1.335 billion on sales of $13.931 billion.

Although his return to Apple as interim CEO generated mixed reactions, Jobs is now widely credited with saving Apple, and the financial markets have resumed their love affair with the company's stock (see Figure 9.3).

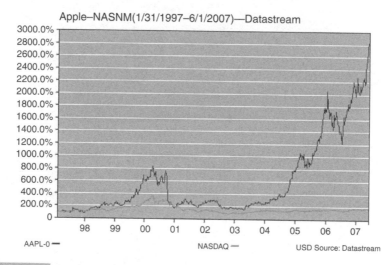

Figure 9.3 A comparison of Apple Computers' stock price performance with the Nasdaq index (1997–2007)

Jobs brought Apple back from the brink of disaster by reconciling the firm with its innovation roots and aligning its technology and business strategies with its historical identity. Jobs seized every communication opportunity to reinforce this theme. One year after his return, for example, he used the official unveiling event of the iMac, the product that epitomizes the new Apple, to dramatize his vision:

If you had just arrived back from Mars from a vacation and you saw this thing, you'd say, 'Whoa, let me guess, could it be…?' And you'd hope it would be Apple Computer. Apple is back to its roots, starting to innovate again.[4]

At the same meeting, Jonathan Ive, Apple's chief of industrial design, concurred: "It's in the genes of this company to be different."[5]

To skeptics who wonder whether Apple's market-leading, highly profitable ventures in online music and consumer electronics may actually be driving the company far from personal computing, Jobs contends:

The great thing is that Apple's DNA hasn't changed...The place where Apple has been standing for the last two decades is exactly where computer technology and the consumer electronics markets are converging. So it's not like we're having to cross the river to go somewhere else; the other side of the river is coming to us.

Whether the Apple of today is actually the same as or different from the Apple of 1976 can be an interesting philosophical question but is not all that consequential. More important is the fact that Jobs has been able to persuade insiders and outsiders alike that Apple has reinhabited its soul after drifting under his predecessors. He has successfully articulated a narrative emphasizing continuity between Apple's past, present, and future and has consistently aligned the company's strategies with the narrative.

Peter Saunders

After two decades of continuous growth and increased profitability, the mid-1990s were trying times for The Body Shop and its cofounders, Anita and Gordon Roddick. Founded in 1976 to sell homemade natural personal care products and with a strong, very visible commitment to social activism, the company had grown into a multinational retail network. But The Body Shop's financial performance lagged behind its social activism.

In particular, the company's initiatives in the U.S. market, begun in 1989, were unprofitable and challenged the foundations of the Roddicks' management philosophy and practices. Anita's political activism and her stance against the first Gulf War alienated franchisees. Her gut rejection of traditional advertising and exclusive reliance on visible social activism to increase public awareness of The Body Shop did not fit the American market, where the competitive environment was very intense. Finally, The Body Shop's initially distinctive holistic formula and emphasis on natural ingredients were quickly imitated by competitors across the globe, thus undermining the company's differentiation strategy.

With a languishing stock price (see Figure 9.4), the Roddicks were under siege. The experiment with putting social responsibility at the heart of business strategy was losing its shine.

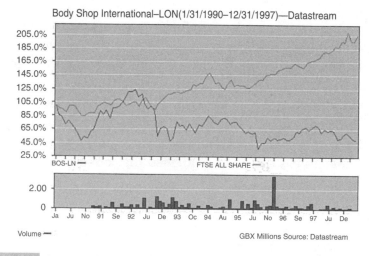

Figure 9.4 A comparison of The Body Shop stock price performance with the FTSE (1990–1997)

The Roddicks' initial reaction was that the stock market did not, and could not, understand how unique The Body Shop was, and they sought to privatize the company.[6] At the time, the Roddicks owned 25 percent of the company and would have had to raise $580.8 million (£380 million) to de-list The Body Shop. This proved to be very difficult; a few months later, they abandoned the idea.

In a statement, Anita Roddick and her husband, Chairman Gordon Roddick, said taking the company private would have saddled it with growth-impairing debt.[7]

The announcement further disappointed investors, and the situation in the United States kept deteriorating ($5.9 million in losses in 1997 and $3.38 million in losses in 1998). With the pressure mounting, Anita Roddick stepped aside, shared the nonexecutive chairman job with her husband, and handed the CEO title to Patrick Gournay, a professional manager hired from Danone. They transferred ownership of the U.S. business to a joint venture with Adrian Bellamy, an American investor who sat on the board of The Body Shop.[8] To turn around the U.S. business, where The Body Shop had 290 of its nearly 1,500 stores, Bellamy hired Peter Saunders, a Canadian with a solid track record in retailing.

The medicine administered by Saunders to the U.S. business delivered some positive results, but the overall performance of The Body Shop remained low and inconsistent, as shown in Figure 9.5. Meanwhile, the Roddicks sought a buyer for the company.[9]

Figure 9.5 A comparison of The Body Shop stock price performance with the FTSE (1998–2001)

The Roddicks realized that they could neither turn around nor sell the company, so in February 2002, they ceded the chairmanship of The Body Shop to Adrian Bellamy, remaining on the board as nonexecutive directors. Peter Saunders, who was until then CEO of U.S. operations, was promoted to CEO of the parent company.[10]

In the four years following the appointment of Peter Saunders, the company's performance improved, and its stock outperformed the London FTSE index (see Figure 9.6).

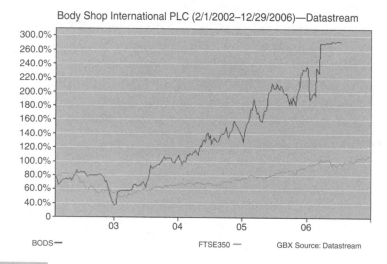

Body Shop International PLC (2/1/2002–12/29/2006)—Datastream

BODS—   FTSE350 —   GBX Source: Datastream

Figure 9.6 A comparison of The Body Shop stock price performance with the FTSE (2002–2006).

Saunders could have sought to redefine the company and its mission, jettisoning its commitment to social activism. Instead, he sought to improve its financial performance by leveraging the company's historical core. Saunders reaffirmed The Body Shop's commitment to social responsibility and continued the company's involvement with and support of social issues. The company's Web site continues to highlight the company's creed: "Against Animal Testing. Support Community Trade. Activate Self-Esteem. Defend Human Rights. Protect Our Planet." Elsewhere in the Web site, one can read the following:

Activism has been part of the DNA of The Body Shop. The past has been a testament to an extraordinary partnership with millions of men, women and children all over the globe. And what about the future? The unique blend of product, passion and partnership that characterizes the story of The Body Shop will continue to evolve. It is a shared vision. So the great experiment goes on.[11]

At the same time that he signaled, internally and externally, his commitment to The Body Shop's unique legacy, Saunders sought to improve its business performance through a differentiation strategy that is in line with its identity. The strategy consists of upgrading The Body Shop's brand and positioning between cheap mass-market brands and highly expensive brands:

Peter Saunders has said that the brand should offer cheaper alternatives to brands such as Estee Lauder, Clinique and Elizabeth Arden. He believes that this will place The Body Shop in a position between the mass and prestige markets.[12]

To implement what he called the "masstige" (mass and prestige) strategy, Saunders updated the product range and renovated the stores to appeal to affluent and mature customers, even though the company's historical success was made by cash-strapped youngsters. As Saunders acknowledged, "If there is any baggage, if that is the right word, it is that it was (a brand) for the young," says Saunders. "I think the teenager of yesterday remembers us of yesterday and has not given us the chance to show we have grown."[13]

Saunders' major achievement is that he was able to update The Body Shop's internal management and external positioning and, at the same time, reaffirm the company's commitment to its roots. In so doing, he avoided the kind of identity clash that characterized John Sculley's leadership at Apple or Carly Fiorina's at HP. The story of The Body Shop illustrates a successful, though rare, transition from founders to professional managers and shows how the latter can create value by leveraging a firm's identity instead of dismantling it. The decision by L'Oréal to run The Body Shop as an independent company after its acquisition in 2006 and to retain Saunders as CEO are further evidence of Saunders' sound approach to the company's *I*Dimension*.

Louis Gerstner

After two decades of undisputed worldwide leadership in the computer industry, IBM found itself struggling in the 1980s as a new generation of technology entrepreneurs took the magic out of mainframes and established the personal computer as a cheaper and more versatile alternative. IBM's once-enviable margins and profits were deteriorating in direct proportion to the PC share of information technology (IT) spending. When he was offered the top job at IBM in the fall of 1984, John Akers did not anticipate the depth and breadth of the problems in the company he had been called upon to lead.

Two years into his tenure, however, the warning signals were intensifying, as the following quote from *Business Week*[14] suggests:

The company has had seven straight quarters of slowing revenue growth and sagging earnings, capped most recently by a 27% drop in third-quarter profits....IBM stock, once the bluest chip of all, has dropped 25% since it hit a high of 161 six months ago. The company's total market value now stands at $75 billion, down from $97 billion back then. A decade ago return on equity was more than twice the average for the Standard & Poor's 500 index. Now it's 1.4 times as big.

In an effort to restore IBM's performance and luster, Akers slashed the workforce, pursued aggressive cost reductions, and reorganized the company into 13 product-based business lines and a global sales business line.[15] Unfortunately, his successive plans did not provide the expected relief, and, as shown in Figure 9.7,

IBM's stock felt the pain and consistently underperformed the S&P 500 during his tenure.

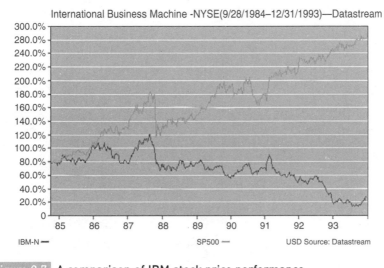

Figure 9.7 **A comparison of IBM stock price performance**

Akers' plan to divide IBM into several "Blue Babies" was halted as the board of directors abruptly removed him from office and handed the reins, in March 1993, to Louis Gerstner, then RJR Nabisco's chairman and CEO. A story in the *Financial Times*[16] summarized the Akers era: nearly 200,000 jobs and $15 billion were lost between 1986 and 1994.

Gerstner's appointment at the helm of IBM was greeted with skepticism. The daily newspaper *The Globe and Mail* captured the general feeling at the time in a vivid headline published the day of Gerstner's appointment, March 26, 1993:

Can a cigarette salesman get IBM smokin'? Opinion is mixed on whether Louis Gerstner has the right stuff to improve Big Blue's stock. He may find some eerie parallels between the troubled fortunes of RJR's chief product, cigarettes, and IBM's, mainframe computers.

The question was legitimate. Gerstner was an outsider stepping into a company that had been managed continuously by insiders raised within its ranks. Moreover, he was a marketer in an industry where a deep understanding of technology was seen as a prerequisite for managing such a large and complex organization as IBM. At the time of his retirement ten years later, and with the benefit of hindsight, there was little doubt about the wisdom of choosing Gerstner to lead the turnaround at IBM. The company's performance had improved dramatically, and Gerstner was seen as the architect of a miraculous transformation:[17]

(Gerstner) took a dispirited, directionless, money-losing collection of businesses and utterly transformed it. As Intel Chairman Andy Grove puts it, "He has done more than I ever imagined anyone could do with that company." The result is a giant that had profits of $7.7 billion last year—more than any tech company other than Microsoft— on sales of $86 billion, almost twice as much as any other tech company and enough to put it in the top ten of the FORTUNE 500.

After trailing the S&P 500 under John Akers, IBM's stock price consistently outperformed the index in the ten years of Gerstner's tenure (see Figure 9.8).

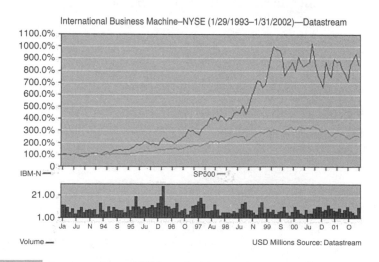

Figure 9.8 A comparison of IBM stock price performance with the S&P 500 (1993–2002)

How did Gerstner achieve what is considered by many observers as a miracle?[18] Commentators and Gerstner[19] have offered different explanations covering the usual range of leadership style, strategic reorientation, organizational redesign, brand management, communication strategy, and financial engineering. Gerstner used all of these to revive IBM, but the key to his success lies in his recognition of the significance of the *I*Dimension*. When he took the reins, IBM was in deep trouble, and he had a variety of options. He could proceed with Akers' plan to dismantle the company. He could seek to remodel IBM after one of the successful young IT companies, such as Dell or Microsoft. He could pursue a merger with another company and dissolve IBM's woes into a larger pot. More radically, he could pull IBM out of the IT sector and sell different portions of the business to companies where they would be more profitable. Finally, he could have been tempted to change the company's name, because IBM had become synonymous with market inertia, technological obsolescence, and mounting losses. Interestingly, though, Gerstner did none of these things. Instead, he sought to cure IBM by showing respect for, and building on, its legacy. Gerstner's choice to fix IBM as it was, instead of changing it into another company, is understandable. The IBM brand was still strong despite all the negative commentary. The company was well respected and present in the large corporate segment. IBM had an unequaled technological portfolio, a committed and competent workforce, and a strong global presence. Instead of scrapping IBM's identity, Gerstner de-emphasized the centrality of mainframes in the internal and external perception of the company. At the same time, he sought to broaden the internal and external understanding of IBM as an integrated provider of IT solutions.[20] Gerstner's biggest achievement was to demonstrate the possibility of large-scale change in continuity. With services contributing, in 2004, about half of the total revenue ($46.213 out of $96.293 billion) and one-third of the gross profits ($11.576 out of $36.032 billion),[21] IBM is back where it was in the early years of computing. In those days, IBM could not sell hardware and software without providing services, because clients did not have the programming capabilities and did not know how to operate computers.

In contrast with the identity big bang orchestrated by Jean-Marie Messier, who sought to kill the Compagnie Générale des Eaux and create a new identity de novo, Gerstner shook IBM's strategy, structure, technologies, and culture profoundly. At the same time, he ensured that, inside and outside, IBM continued to be perceived as "Big Blue," a blue-chip, reliable company.

Carlos Ghosn

In 1999, Louis Schweitzer, then chairman and CEO of the French automaker Renault, risked $5.4 billion for a controlling stake (37 percent) in the Japanese Nissan Motors. At that time, Nissan was nearing default on a $20 billion debt, its market value was sinking (see Figure 9.9), and bankruptcy was hanging over the once-admired symbol of Japanese industrial supremacy.

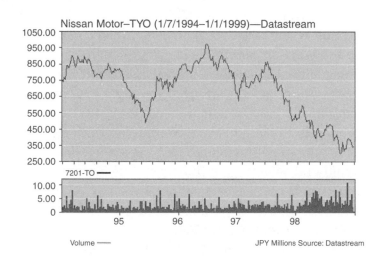

Figure 9.9 Nissan Motors stock price performance (1994–1999)

In 2005, Nissan was one of the most profitable automakers
in the world, with an operating profit margin of more than
10 percent,[22] and its stock price reached mind-boggling heights
(see Figure 9.10). Due to Louis Schweiter's bet-the-company
stroke, Renault has become a key and profitable[23] player in the
global car industry.

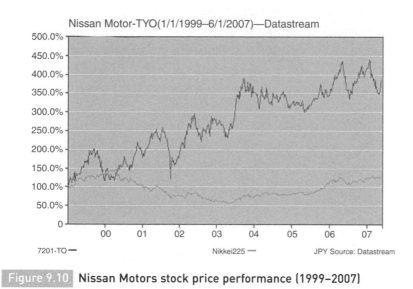

Nissan Motor-TYO(1/1/1999–6/1/2007)—Datastream

7201-TO ▬   Nikkei225 ▬   JPY Source: Datastream

Figure 9.10 Nissan Motors stock price performance (1999–2007)

Carlos Ghosn, the man dispatched by Louis Schweitzer to fix
Nissan, is considered a modern-day hero. Renault's investment
and Ghosn's appointment were met with the same kind of
skepticism expressed when Steve Jobs returned to Apple and
Louis Gerstner was appointed at IBM. Ghosn had many liabilities
to overcome, and the odds were against him. Many doubted
whether a recently privatized French carmaker could rescue and
manage a nearly bankrupt Japanese company.[24] Ghosn had never
been first in command at the top of a large company, and his
credentials at the time were those of a "cost killer," a
competence honed at the tire maker Michelin and successfully

transferred to Renault. Moreover, Ghosn's appointment as chief operating officer reporting to then-chairman Yoshikazu Hanawa left many wondering how much freedom and authority he would have to execute his plans. On many counts, Ghosn's revival of Nissan is as impressive as the achievements of Steve Jobs at Apple and Louis Gerstner at IBM.

While Ghosn and the Franco-Japanese management team he assembled to assist him performed radical surgery on Nissan, they were very careful not to jeopardize the firm's identity. In explaining the turnaround, Ghosn has emphasized consistently how he sought to change Nissan and preserve its identity at the same time. He wrote in a *Harvard Business Review* article[25] that:

In corporate turnarounds, particularly those related to mergers or alliances, success is not simply a matter of making fundamental changes to a company's organization and operations. *You also have to protect the company's identity and the self-esteem of its people.*[26]... As might be expected, given the cutbacks we made in Japan, the public was initially uneasy about the revival plan, and I took a lot of the flak as the foreigner in charge. Inside Nissan, though, people recognized that we weren't trying to take the company over but rather were attempting to restore it to its former glory. We had the trust of employees for a simple reason: We had shown them respect. Although we were making many profound changes in the way Nissan carried out its *business*, we were always careful to protect Nissan's identity and its dignity as a company.

This statement shows that Ghosn has a deep understanding of how a manager can earn respect from people by showing respect for their sense of who they are and what their common house— their firm—stands for. Persuading insiders and outsiders that he wanted to help Nissan become the innovative Japanese car company that it had been before made it easier for him to rally employees and partners around this goal and to gain their acceptance of painful sacrifices.

Endnotes

1. *Fortune,* November 9, 1998: "The Second Coming of Apple."

2. *Fortune,* July 26, 1993: "Odd Man Out: John Sculley Steps Down as Apple CEO."

3. *Fortune,* March 3, 1997: "Something's Rotten in Cupertino."

4. *Business Week,* May 25, 1998: "Back to the Future at Apple."

5. Ibid.

6. The *Wall Street Journal,* November 1, 1995: "Body Shop Shares Jump on Reports It Will Go Private."

7. The *Wall Street Journal,* March 5, 1996: "Body Shop Chief Abandons Plans to Take Firm Private."

8. The *Wall Street Journal,* May 13, 1998: "Body Shop Founder Roddick Steps Aside as CEO."

9. The *New York Times,* June 8, 2001: "Body Shop Is in Talks on Sale to Mexican Company."

10. The *New York Times,* February 13, 2002: "Body Shop's Founders Give Up Control."

11. From www.thebodyshop.com.

12. *Design Week,* July 8, 2004: "Time to Shape Up at the Body Shop."

13. *Retail Week,* October 22, 2004: "Rebuilding a Brand on Perfume, Not Politics."

14. *Business Week*, November 17, 1998: "How IBM Is Fighting Back—To Reignite Growth, It's Undergoing Toughest Self-Scrutiny in Years."

15. The *New York Times*, December 21, 1992: "IBM's Next Remodeling Could Be a Doozy."

16. *Financial Times,* November 12, 2002: "How Big Blue Came Back from the Brink."

17. *Fortune,* February 18, 2002: "The Future of IBM—Lou Gerstner Seems to Have Pulled off a Miracle. Sam Palmisano Will Have to Be at Least as Good."

18. Ibid.

19. Gerstner, L. 2002. *Who Says Elephants Can't Dance? Inside IBM's Historic Turnaround,* New York, NY: HarperCollins.

20. The following quote from *Business Week*, September 13, 1992, uses different words to convey the same idea: "The essence of Gerstner's work (was) the transformation of IBM from a computer company to a technology and services company in which the Internet plays a key role."

21. Source: www.ibm.com.

22. Nissan's operating income was at 10.04 percent in 2005, 11.10 percent in 2004, and 10.80 percent in 2003. In the same period, Toyota's operating income stood at 8.76 percent, 9.02 percent, and 8.49 percent. (Source: Thomson One Banker.)

23. At the beginning of 2006, Renault owned 44 percent of Nissan. In 2004, Nissan contributed $1.77 billion to Renault's record-high profits of $4.5 billion.

24. Bob Lutz, now vice chairman of General Motors, is reported to have said that Renault would have made better use of the $5.7bn by buying gold bars, putting them in a container, and sinking them in the sea.

25. Ghosn, C. 2002. "Saving the Business Without Losing the Company," *Harvard Business Review*, 80(1).

26. The emphasis in the quote is added by the authors.

Diagnosing Your Firm's Identity

How can you get a handle on the *I*Dimension* of your organization? As you saw in Chapter 2, identity can be an extraordinary asset for a firm; however, as shown in Chapter 3, identity can also become a serious liability. Furthermore, although there can be convergence internally and externally about a given firm's identity, there can also be divergence.

To avoid becoming a casualty of the *I*Dimension,* you need some idea of where your firm is located along these dimensions. To what extent is there convergence, both internally and externally, about your firm's identity?

Because identity lies deep in an organization's consciousness and is rarely subject to reflection and open debate, it is more difficult to get a handle on than are, for example, its strategies, structures, processes, and systems, all of which can be inferred from visible actions and activities. Discovering or pinpointing a firm's identity is a real challenge, best met through conducting what we call an *identity audit.* And because carrying out a thorough identity audit is a demanding exercise, we begin this chapter with a discussion of the circumstances that call for one and the kinds of benefits you might expect from this investment.

Who Needs an Identity Audit?

The implication of the taken-for-granted nature of identity is that most organizations and their managers are rarely led to establish connections between the identity of their firm and some issues at hand. Instead, they typically frame these issues with reference to the firm's manifest dimensions and seek to fix them. When they feel a need for outside assistance, managers tend to instinctively call in management consultants with expertise on the dimensions where they sense problems are located.

Like most managers, most consultants are not sensitized to the *I*Dimension.* They define their engagement in what has become the standard way, producing data-driven reports that identify gaps between actual and desired states, and recommending remedial action. This approach can deliver results in situations where the proposed changes do not intentionally or unintentionally call the client's identity into question. It is problematic, however, if the changes do call the client's identity into question. The need to assess a firm's identity arises when, as in the case of Polaroid, it experiences persistent performance problems that cannot be fixed through identity-neutral initiatives, or when recently appointed managers introduce changes in the firm's manifest dimensions that, intentionally or unintentionally, potentially threaten the firm's current identity.

Because most managers are either unaware of the *I*Dimension* or are unwilling to address it head-on, the opportunity for an identity audit most often arises in the process of working on some strategic or operational issues. To illustrate how senior managers more often than not are unaware of the *I*Dimension* and its significance, consider the following example taken from a large French company. The company had been operating for four decades in North America, through several acquisitions, and had become an industry leader in the United States. Senior management at the company's Paris headquarters were frustrated by the slow and problematic pace of integration of the North American operations into the parent company. We were asked by the company's chief executive officer to help him and his team understand impediments to integration. We interviewed more than 30 senior managers from France, the United States, and Canada who had been involved with the North American operations. Initial discussions with top management revolved around technical and cultural topics. Later interviews revealed that the technical and cultural issues encountered throughout four decades of engagement in North America were actually symptoms of deeper tensions in the identity of the French parent. Although our feedback to the management team was initially surprising to them, it brought to the surface a number of issues that all members of the team had felt for some time but had never addressed collectively. For example, we showed the management team that their unquestioned view of the firm as an "integrated industrial company" was the source of some of the problems encountered in North America. Being an integrated industrial company entailed tight coordination across the company's businesses throughout the world, but North American managers never saw the economic benefits of coordinating their local strategies with those of business units in Europe or Asia. This proved to be a major fault line in the internal definition of the company's identity, which, if not addressed, would have led to continued problems of integration.

A consulting project carried out by a team of participants from the ESSEC Business School Executive MBA[1] with AFAT Voyages, a French network of independent travel agents, provides another example of how the need for identity audit may arise in the process of a traditional strategic diagnosis and planning exercise. The project's initial brief called for an assessment of the network's strategic position and the identification of revenue growth opportunities. As the team carried out interviews with network members and clients, they realized that the identity of AFAT Voyages was unclear both internally and externally. Building on this feedback, the team reported to the steering committee that the elaboration of a growth strategy required clarification of the network's mission, which required a deeper investigation into what the network meant to its members and other constituencies. The steering committee agreed with the recommendation and authorized the team to perform an identity audit.

The decision to undertake an identity audit may be stimulated by major events or discontinuities that bring identity to the attention of managers. At SSL-International, for example, managers' awareness of, and interest in, the *I*Dimension* was dictated by the need to bind together three firms with different heritages. At Conecto,[2] a Norwegian collection agency, the decision to undertake an identity audit was made in response to the rapid growth of the company. The founders, two former police officers, wanted to show that debt collection could be conducted in an ethical, humane way and sought to infuse these values in the DNA of the firm. As the company grew, the founders felt a need to articulate its identity more clearly for clients, debtors, and recent hires to ensure that it remained faithful to its roots and did not drift into a classical debt collection firm.[3] The audit was conducted by a team of researchers who were able to involve employees and external stakeholders in a deep-dive exercise that delivered a clear articulation of the company's identity.

Discovering Identity: A Generic Approach

To illustrate the discovery of a company's identity, it is useful to begin with the kind of questioning that can bring to the surface the identity of an individual. To discover your own identity, you can begin by considering objective and visible attributes, such as your gender, marital status, ethnic background, age, nationality, profession, and/or employer. For example, because you are a manager, it would seem logical to consider this an important indicator of your sense of who you are. However, you may object that being a manager is just something you do for a living and that your sense of yourself is elsewhere. You may view yourself, foremost, as a compassionate Christian, an entrepreneur, a caring parent, an inveterate biker, a loving spouse, or any combination of these. The first lesson here is that you cannot know who you are from merely compiling observable facts. To know who you are, you need access to your subjective sense of yourself.

How do you access your subjective sense of yourself? Had you thought of yourself as a caring parent before you declined the highly attractive job that would have moved the family overseas and disturbed your children's schooling and social lives? Or, would you have defined yourself as a compassionate Christian before you had to deal with the human implications of a downsizing plan? Or, how much did your American citizenship mean to your self-understanding before 9/11? The second lesson is that some aspects of your identity lie deep in your subconscious and are not revealed before issues and circumstances bring them to the surface. Thus, to get a sense of your identity, an exploration of your life history is needed to see how you behaved in a variety of situations. Because some identity anchors may not be revealed through a study of your past, it would be necessary to submit you to a series of hypothetical situations and ask you how you would react and why. For example, parenthood may come up as more important to you than career advancement if you were asked what you would do if offered a professional opportunity that would severely reduce the time spent with your children. In sum, to uncover your personal identity anchors, we need to do the following:

1. Take as a starting point a number of objective, externally observable attributes that have a good chance of participating in your self-concept: gender, profession, education, nationality, family status, faith, and so forth.

2. Ask you to define yourself. Through this definition, we can collect insights about identity anchors that are not externally available and, perhaps, de-emphasize some objective attributes that are not relevant to your self-understanding.

3. Observe your past behavior over a time frame long enough to give us a better understanding of who you are through your reactions in a number of identity-revealing circumstances.

4. Complement the emerging picture, when necessary, by submitting you to a series of hypothetical situations where you would have to make decisions and choices that would reflect your sense of who you are.

The outcome of this process is a list of anchors that, together, would represent your self-concept. Some of these anchors are visible from the outside; some, though not externally visible, belong to your consciousness; and still others lie deep in your unconsciousness.

Some anchors, of course, may conflict with others. For example, being an "effective marketing manager" *and* a "caring parent" can be in conflict because your job involves introducing as many kids as possible to smoking your company's cigarette brands. Although the marketing manager side of you is proud of your ingenious new smoker recruitment campaigns, the caring parent side tells you that what you are doing is wrong.

Assuming that we were able to spend enough time observing and listening to you to elicit your sense of who you are, can we say that we know your identity? The truth is that our job is incomplete, because we do not know how you are viewed by the people around you. Assume, for example, that you are a female manager working in a predominantly male organization. You do not care much about gender and give your profession more weight in your self-definition, but your supervisor, your colleagues, or your clients may primarily see you as a woman. In this case, it would be more difficult to ascertain your definition of yourself. Inevitably, the gap between how you define yourself and how you are defined by others generates misunderstandings, distorted expectations, and frustrations. Without some alignment between your inner and external identities, your interactions with people surrounding you would be extremely complicated. If this alignment is important to you, the collection of information about how you are viewed by the people you interact with on a regular basis is required, as in 360 feedback exercises.

We can conclude, then, that your personal identity

- Cannot be known by looking at easily observable features only.
- Is defined by some anchors that you may not initially be aware of.
- May be composed of anchors that are contradictory.
- May be seen differently by others than by you.
- May not be seen in the same way by all others.

The exercise of surfacing an individual's identity provides some clues as to how to uncover a firm's identity, along with some indication of how tricky the exercise can be. First, you can take clues from externally observable aspects, such as the firm's core business, customer base, nationality, or ownership structure. For example, it may be assumed that the mode of ownership or the sector where it participates are important identity anchors for a firm. Remember, however, that making inferences about inner identity from externally observable aspects can be misleading and that discovering identity requires deeper exploration. Therefore, closer observation of your firm is necessary to validate initial assumptions and discover identity anchors that are not visible from the outside. By doing this, we may confirm that the ownership mode is considered internally as an important identity anchor for your firm but the sector is not. Public statements about your firm are one source of information about identity. These may take the form of a mission statement, a list of values, a corporate history, or other kinds of written materials that directly or indirectly specify what makes the firm unique among all other firms or among its competitors. For example, Ben & Jerry's view of itself as a socially responsible business is a central part of its identity. It was clearly articulated by the founders at the company's inception, has remained central, and is visible on the company's Web site and in other written communications.

Certainly, claims about what makes a firm unique cannot be taken at face value, because they can be unsubstantiated or outright misleading. For example, just because senior managers define their organization as a team, a family, or a socially responsible firm does not mean that this is the case in practice. These claims may be more aspirational than realized. Public statements should therefore be treated as hypotheses to be tested in the process of the identity audit. We are confident about the centrality of social responsibility to the identity of Ben & Jerry's not only because this is proclaimed on its Web site, but because the company has consistently behaved in a manner that one would expect of a socially responsible firm.

To continue the audit process, we will find that some identity anchors may be publicly articulated and empirically testable, and other anchors may never have been explicitly articulated. To discover these anchors, we would need to examine a series of past decisions and choices and see what they can tell us about the self-concept of your firm. For example, by studying a series of decisions about new products, we may realize that its identity is not anchored in technology, per se, but in a customer-centric approach to technology, as is the case of Bang & Olufsen.

Close exploration of the subject firm may also reveal potentially inconsistent identity anchors.[4] For example, the firm may be collectively viewed as a global company and as a family business at the same time. Guided by the view of the firm as a global company, top management is sincerely committed to building a global organizational structure and to developing an international management team. However, being a family business, the firm is run by a small, tight-knit group of people with close ties. Thus, the firm is subject to two conflicting identity anchors. As a result, we would expect members of the inner circle (owners and top managers) to feel that foreigners do not understand the company and are not truly committed to it. Foreign managers, on the other hand, would typically complain about the inner circle's inability to understand what it is to be a global company and the lack of advancement opportunities for people who do not belong to the inner circle.

Finally, there may be discrepancies between how insiders (owners, managers, and employees) view the firm and how other stakeholders (customers, analysts, bankers, prospective employees, activist groups) may view it. For example, its managers and employees may view the firm as a progressive employer, while the general public may view it primarily as a polluter. The example of Degussa, discussed in the Introduction to this book, illustrates discrepancies between a firm's inner and external identities. Although the managers and employees of Degussa view it as a different entity from the Degussa of World War II, its opponents challenged this view and claimed that it is the same as the supplier of the deadly Zyklon-B gas used in Nazi concentration camps.

After sorting out visible and revealing invisible identity anchors, the next task is to use this knowledge as a key to understanding what is going on in your firm—economic performance, strategic and operational issues, internal and external conflicts, and impediments to and levers for change. Knowledge about identity would be useless unless it can lead to a better understanding of what goes on in the firm. For example, the identity audit may discover that the firm's diversification strategy has never been successful, because its identity remains strongly anchored in its traditional core business. We may also realize that, despite significant investments abroad, internationalization has been a constant source of difficulties because the firm remains deeply committed to an unspoken, but nevertheless deeply rooted, national identity as French or Japanese or American.

Examples of Identity Audits

To illustrate the general approach just described, we provide three examples of partial identity audits performed by the authors in three different executive training programs.

Consum Electro Corp. (CES): An Old Lady Who Needs Rejuvenation

CES is a multinational company operating in consumer electronics. Participants in a training program for 30 high-potential managers, drawn from different European countries, were asked to describe the company in 2000 and how it should look in 2010. By asking the respondents to think about the changes they want to see in the company in ten years, the exercise leads them to focus on those really important aspects in which change can necessitate a long time frame. The results of the exercise are summarized in Table 10.1.

Table 10.1 What CES Is and Should Be

In 2000, CES Is	In 2010, CES Should Be
German[5]	Global
Male-dominated	Women-friendly
Old organization	Young organization
Hardware company	Software/services company
An industrial firm	A brand
"Old" economy	"New" economy

Although the sample is relatively small for a company employing about 200,000 people at the time of the survey, the answers described quite well the main tensions at work in the identity of CES. Although the company's operations were truly international, its top management was still dominated by homegrown males. The company had clearly noticed the increasing role of software in electronics and was trying hard to cope with this trend, but it was still deeply caught in a view of itself as a manufacturer of electronics hardware. Finally, many people inside the company were still proud of the industrial and engineering prowess of CES, while others wanted the company to think of itself as a brand and to focus more on marketing and delivering value to customers.

Pay TV Corp. (PTC): A Threatened Identity in Need of Conservation

PTC is known in Europe as a pioneer in Pay TV with an innovative and unconventional mind-set. Participants in a training program for high-potential managers were asked about their present view of the firm and how it should evolve in the future (see Table 10.2).

Table 10.2 What PTC Is and Should Be

PTC Is	PTC Should Be
A German[6] or European company	A multicultural company
A Pay TV company	A full media company
A large market leader	A global leader
A creative (special) company	A keeper of the creative spirit
A technology leader	A technology leader
Content-oriented	Customer-focused
Movies and sports	More sports and movies
An informal organization	Less bureaucratic
A family	A family

The answers reveal two contradictory themes. On the one hand, the respondents wanted PTC to become multicultural, global, multimedia, and customer-centric. On the other hand, they wanted to preserve the historical creative, informal, and family aspects of the firm. To understand why these themes express identity tensions at PTC, it should be specified that the survey was conducted in the year following the firm's acquisition by a large media and entertainment conglomerate. The acquisition is known to have provoked anxieties at PTC, whose employees and managers feared the loss of the company's historical identity.

Health-Consumer Co. (HCC): How to Make One Out of Many

HCC is the result of the merger of three companies operating in the health-care and consumer products sectors. Members of the top management team were asked, during a workshop, to answer the questions about what HCC is and what it should be (see Table 10.3).

Table 10.3 What HCC Is and Should Be

Our Firm Is	Our Firm Should Be
A diverse health-care company	A consistently successful company
Branded health care	A health-care brand developer
Confused	From art collector to gardener
A mixed bag	A socially aware company
A confusing mixture of demoralized and overconfident/complacent people	An innovative company
A mixed up, confused adolescent with potential	A company that promotes honesty, openness, excitement, meets customers' needs, strategic thinking, self-support, and fun
International	
Three health-care businesses that have not fused	
A triangle trying to become a circle	
Two lethargic brands	

The answers show how difficult it was for many members of the top management team to define their company in a positive way. It should be added that the workshop was part of an executive training program, whereby the CEO sought to bring together senior and midlevel managers from the three merged firms for the purpose of creating a common identity to which they all could relate.

A Methodological Guide for Conducting an Identity Audit

Whether it is undertaken explicitly for this purpose or arises in the process of dealing with other types of issues, uncovering the identity of an organization requires conducting a methodical search for the more or less clear, shared, and consistent answers to the following questions:

- What is our identity? (What do our people and external stakeholders think is the essence of our company?)

- What is the degree of convergence internally on, and commitment to, this identity?

- What is the degree of consistency between internal and external perceptions of our identity?

- To what extent is our identity an asset? A liability?

- Is our identity enabling us to keep up with external change? Will it in the future?

- Are there internal or external signals that our identity might be blinding us to technological or market trends or structural performance problems?

- Can we go on as *who we are,* or do we need to break away from our identity?

- Who would be threatened and who would be served by a change in our identity?

To answer these questions, this section provides a set of tools that can be used together or selectively for a systematic exploration of a firm's identity.

Exploiting Secondary Sources

The first step in an identity audit is using available internal and external writings about the firm. Internal resources include mission statements, proclamations of the firm's values and beliefs, letters to shareholders, annual reports, speeches given by key stakeholders about the firm (owners, senior managers, union leaders, politicians), unofficial publications, and Web sites fed by employees or their representatives. A careful reading of these resources can help the identity auditor identify recurring themes in how the firm is presented publicly. For example, a systematic exploitation of annual reports and accompanying letters to shareholders revealed a consistent commitment by the founder and his successors to a view of Moulinex as "a French, industrial, innovative, and international company operating in the small-appliance sector." This view of Moulinex was systematically invoked to justify major management decisions and preferences such as the preservation of plants and jobs in France, the refusal to diversify out of small appliances, and the reluctance to transfer manufacturing to lower-cost countries.

Internal resources can and, where possible, should be usefully complemented by outside resources such as news articles and monographs about the firm. When a corporate history is available, it can provide valuable insights about the early life of an organization and show how the founders shaped, more or less consciously, the firm's identity. In our work with the large French firm facing integration issues with its North American operations, we drew on a well-documented corporate history published by a retired senior executive.

Written materials should be exploited with a critical eye, however, and they should never be relied on alone for understanding a firm's identity. To gain a full appreciation of a firm's identity, the auditor must undertake a deeper exploration.

Interviews with Key Constituencies

Through initial discussions with senior managers and a first round of readings about the firm, the auditor must be able to create a list of relevant constituencies whose views of the firm and, more importantly, behavior vis-à-vis the firm are of critical importance. Typically, the list of constituencies includes employees, customers, share owners, suppliers, strategic partners, union leaders, journalists, and financial analysts. In some cases, the question of who matters in defining a firm's identity can yield surprising answers. For example, a brainstorming session with the management team of a company mentioned earlier identified "potential acquisition targets" as an important constituency, because the company was being prepared to undertake a growth strategy through acquisitions. How the company would be viewed by potential acquisition targets was logically considered as important to the success of that strategy.

After mapping key constituencies, the identity auditor must carry out interviews with selected representatives of each group. To capture interviewees' understanding of the focal firm's identity, the auditor can ask them to elaborate about how and why the firm behaved in particular circumstances (extraordinary events, crises, critical incidents, or major decisions). As they provide accounts of what happened and of the firm's behavior, interviewees reveal their view of the firm and its identity. In the case of the large French firm operating in North America, we systematically asked interviewees to elaborate on a series of critical events and incidents that occurred along the company's push to grow in North America. The responses consistently offered explanations that reflected what they believed were core and enduring aspects of the firm.

To reach a more exhaustive understanding of the organization's identity, the auditor may ask interviewees to imagine how their firm would make choices in a series of hypothetical circumstances. In elaborating on how their firm would behave in these circumstances, interviewees would deliver additional insights about its identity.

At the end of each interview, the auditor should have collected answers to the following questions:

- What are the company's most essential, enduring, and distinctive aspects?

- How are these aspects serving or hurting the company's viability, growth, and performance?

- How much is an interviewee personally in alignment or in conflict with the company as it is, and why?

- How should the company evolve in the future to better seize opportunities or cope with challenges?

At the end of this stage, the auditor can map out how relevant stakeholders define and appraise the firm's identity (see Table 10.4).

Table 10.4 Mapping Out the *I*Dimension*

	Perceived Identity Anchors	Appraisal of the Firm's Identity Anchors	Degree of Alignment with the Firm's Identity	Desired Future Changes in the Firm's Identity
Stakeholder group 1				
Stakeholder group 2				
Stakeholder group *n*				

Survey of Stakeholders

The qualitative insights gained through secondary sources and interviews can be used as hypotheses to be confirmed in a large-scale survey of the firm's stakeholders. The questionnaire would contain the following sections:

1. Background information about the respondents.

2. Statements about the firm's identity that respondents must rate on a quantitative scale. For example, respondents can be asked how much they agree with the following statements: "This is a global firm" or "This is a socially responsible firm."

3. For each statement about the firm's identity, respondents should be asked to rate the following items:

   a. This aspect of the firm is an asset or a liability.

   b. I feel in alignment or in conflict with this aspect of the firm.

   c. How easy or difficult would it be to change this aspect of the firm?

4. Assembling the puzzle and making a sense of identity.

A well-executed identity audit should provide managers with a clear mapping of the firm's identity and show where relevant stakeholders stand vis-à-vis this identity. The identity audit is most useful when it brings to the surface unspoken tensions and contradictions in the firm's identity and when it helps managers develop a new perspective on the firm's situation and issues. This perspective cannot be produced through traditional strategy and operations audits. A good identity audit must show managers the following:

1. How much can they or should they draw on the firm's current identity to drive change?

2. What aspects of the firm's identity need to be modified to enable strategic and organizational change that would not be possible within the current identity envelope?

3. If change in identity is required, what identity anchors can managers lean on to introduce change in other anchors?

4. Who will be their allies in the change process, and where should they anticipate resistance?

Endnotes

1. The team worked with AFAT Voyages in 2003 under the supervision of one of the coauthors.

2. The true name of the company cannot be revealed.

3. Brønn, P.S., A. Engell, and H. Martinsen. 2006. "A Reflective Approach to Uncovering Actual Identity," *European Journal of Marketing,* 40(7/8): 886–901.

4. Think again about Europe. Some people think that Europe is a geographic area. Others believe that Europe's identity is defined by Christianity. Still others think that Europe's identity lies in humanistic ideals. These three views were brought into the spotlight by the debates surrounding the drafting and adoption of the constitutional treaty.

5. This is not the firm's true nationality.

6. This is not the true nationality of PTC.

Leading in the Age of Identity

The fundamental premise of this book is that we now find ourselves in the Age of Identity, an age in which identity issues are ubiquitous—at the individual, organizational, and societal levels. In all spheres of activity, and particularly in business, leaders who are aware of the significance of identity for their firm—either instinctively or through systematic investigation—have a distinct advantage over those who are not aware. Imagine a case in which two leaders are equally creative strategists, equally skilled in the management of operations, and equally tuned in to the needs and priorities of their customers. But one is sensitive to the *I*Dimension,* and the other is not. Our research strongly suggests that the former will be more successful in her career than the latter, and that the gap is widening. As identity issues become increasingly pervasive, the need for sophisticated leaders who understand how to manage through identity will multiply. These leaders can leverage their awareness either to further reinforce their firm's identity when conditions so warrant or to alter their firm's current identity when it constrains performance or adaptive capacity.

This chapter discusses the leadership challenges in each scenario, starting with how leaders can reinforce the *I*Dimension* and then what is required to change it. To set up this discussion, we will look at the recent leadership history at 3M. In December of 2000, James McNerney, a veteran GE executive who was passed over as Jack Welch's successor, was named CEO of the company. He was the first outsider to hold the top position in the company's history. His mandate was to breathe new life into a company that had a reputation for innovation but whose performance in the 1990s had slipped noticeably. McNerney acted quickly, eliminating jobs, cutting costs, and introducing GE's Six Sigma program to boost efficiency and eliminate defects in the production process. His actions were straight out of the GE playbook. The company's stock price improved, and the discipline he introduced seemed to be paying off. But this was 3M, not GE.

In 2005, McNerney left 3M for the top job at Boeing. Reflecting on McNerney's departure, Brian Hindo wrote in *Business Week*:[1]

. . . his successors face a challenging question: whether the relentless emphasis on efficiency had made 3M a less creative company. That's a vitally important issue for a company whose very identity is built on innovation.

The Board evidently concluded that 3M's historical commitment to innovation needed to be reaffirmed, and they appointed George Buckley, a Ph.D. chemical engineer, to succeed McNerney. Since moving into the position, Buckley has been attempting to rekindle the passion for innovation that characterized the company in earlier years.

The changes at the top of 3M help illustrate the connections between leadership and the *I*Dimension*. McNerney, a 3M outsider, was able to institute a series of changes at the company that enhanced efficiency and financial performance, but the changes were at odds with the company's identity. He obviously believed that deep change was necessary. But did he cut too deep? Did the changes he made fundamentally alter the *I*Dimension* at 3M? His departure leaves that very much an open question, but the actions of his successor certainly suggest that many inside the company felt that something important had been taken away. Will 3M be able to recapture its former creativity and reestablish its reputation as an innovator? Only time will tell. But the example illustrates the kinds of trade-offs that leaders and boards who choose leaders must face as they move forward.

Reinforcing the *I*Dimension*

When managers believe that the current identity of the firm is a key asset, they can contribute to its reinforcement through both symbolic and substantive actions. Symbolic reinforcement of identity can be achieved through positive discourse about what makes the firm unique, collective events at various levels of scale, and involvement in the larger community. Positive discourse about identity can be made through speeches and the production and dissemination, inside and outside the firm, of literature emphasizing and eulogizing the firm's uniqueness. To show and share their awareness of the organization's identity, managers can organize various kinds of gatherings for employees or external stakeholders so that they can feel how special the organization in question is. Finally, they can promote their firm's identity through involvement in or sponsorship of highly visible initiatives or events that fit well with the firm's sense of itself and how it is viewed by outsiders. There is no magic to these activities. In fact, most companies commonly engage in some form of them. But what they should avoid is reinforcing the *I*Dimension* when change rather than continuity is what is called for.

Although symbolic reinforcement is useful and necessary to remind employees and outside constituents about a firm's special character, it is not enough to sustain the firm's identity in the long run. To substantiate claims about what distinguishes their firm from others, managers need to prove that they are faithful to that identity in their concrete decisions and actions. This may be reflected through decisions made about people: recruitment, promotion, compensation, or layoffs. Managers can also show their personal alignment with a firm's identity by making strategic and operating decisions that are consistent with the firm's sense of itself. This is clearly what George Buckley is doing at 3M.

In the absence of substantive action, symbolic promotion of a firm's identity can be perceived as mere lip service and can hamper a leader's effectiveness. Carly Fiorina at HP, and John Sculley before her at Apple, ignored this principle at a high personal cost. They both lauded the firms they were brought in to manage and the legacies left by the founders, but their subsequent decisions and actions suggested otherwise and were interpreted both internally and externally as being at odds with their initial discourse. Are we implying that every leader has to bow to a firm's inherited identity and align him- or herself with it? Our answer is clearly "no," and we will elaborate on this point in the following section. Our point here is about being honest and consistent. When leaders want people, both inside and outside the firm, to believe that the firm's identity is a key asset, they must give tangible proof that they believe what they preach.

Reinforcing an established identity does not necessarily mean maintaining the status quo. Carlos Ghosn, Steve Jobs, and Peter Saunders, three masters of the *I*Dimension* profiled in Chapter 9, show how recognition of and respect for a firm's identity can help a leader garner internal and external support for major changes in a firm's strategy and operations.

As paradoxical as this might sound, the paradox is only apparent, for the *I*Dimension* is not necessarily tied to every concrete aspect of the firm. Unless a given dimension is deemed essential by particularly influential internal or external stakeholders, it can be changed without provoking change in the *I*Dimension* itself. A leader can, for example, close an operation or a particular product line that is not considered essential to the firm's identity. This type of decision naturally will be resisted by those who stand to lose something in the process. However, as long as the decision does not jeopardize the heart and soul of the firm, opposition will remain circumscribed, and other stakeholders will have little or no incentive to add their voice to those of the dissenters. Leaders who can make a compelling case that, as painful as they can be, some changes are needed to preserve or better reflect the firm's identity can develop allies and enhance the legitimacy of their decisions.

By emphasizing his awareness of and respect for the identity of Nissan, Carlos Ghosn was given the benefit of the doubt and was able to put the company through far-reaching strategic and operational change. Steve Jobs shook up Apple profoundly and explained that he did so for the sake of reconciling the firm with its innovative roots. In a different way, Peter Saunders introduced significant changes at The Body Shop and was eager to communicate his respect for the unique identity bestowed on the firm by its founders.

Although these examples show that a good deal of change can be achieved within the boundaries of a firm's *I*Dimension,* not every desirable or necessary change is possible within a firm's extant identity envelope. There are contexts in which leaders cannot change some strategic or operational aspects of the firm without calling its identity into question, either deliberately or unintentionally. In these contexts, leaders sensitive to the importance of *I*Dimension* should focus on reconfiguring the firm's identity in a way that makes the necessary changes possible.

Dealing with Identity and Identification at Individual and Group Levels

In the Introduction to this book, we characterized the Age of Identity as an era in which individuals and groups are proactively involved in defining who they are and how they want others to see them. We also stressed that today's leaders must be aware of this trend and ensure that the organizations they lead have clear, consistent, and, more importantly, functional identities. But just as they must seek purposefully to manage the identity of the organization and promote identification with it, leaders must not forget that the human beings who work for or interact with the organization are also busy defining and asserting individual and group identities, such as gender, ethnicity, age group, lifestyle, or personal hobbies. These identities, while largely beyond management influence, should not be ignored in the workplace.

The ensuing challenge for managers is to work simultaneously to establish and reinforce an overarching identity for the organization and to rally internal and external audiences around it. At the same time, managers must accept and support the existence of diverse identities and identifications in their organization. To square the circle, managers need to ensure that the identity of the organization is precise enough to express how it is different from all others. Yet that identity must also be broad enough to enable individuals and groups whose social identities may be anchored in a variety of dimensions to see the whole and to identify with the organization they work for or deal with. In the Age of Identity, to be resilient and generate feelings of identification and loyalty, an organization must provide an environment in which individuals can define themselves in any way they please and, at the same time, identify with and take pride in working for, buying from, or investing in that particular organization. In these organizations, good organizational citizenship and self-realization are not mutually exclusive, as they may be in some organizations, but rather are compatible and mutually supportive.

When the *I*Dimension* Must Change

Ask a senior executive what it means to change a firm's identity, and he or she will most likely talk about redesigning the logo and visual materials and, occasionally, changing the company's name. Changing the **I*Dimension** sometimes involves what many consultants and marketing specialists usually call *corporate identity change* or *corporate rebranding,* but the two processes are different. To use a familiar image, corporate identity change or rebranding is analogous to changing an individual's physical appearance by changing the clothing or makeup the person wears, cosmetic surgery, and, in extreme cases, by changing the individual's name. By contrast, changing the **I*Dimension** reaches much deeper, to the heart and soul of an individual, and does not necessarily require altering the individual's appearance. Although the two types of change may sometimes support each other, it is important that managers be aware of their differences and, more importantly, that they do not use one type of change in the pursuit of results that can only be delivered by the other type.

Managers who are satisfied with the configuration of internal and external beliefs about the essence of the firm can still see the value of updating, every few years, its corporate skin. On the other hand, managers who seek to change the **I*Dimension** need to address deeply rooted views of the firm and do not necessarily have to change its physical appearance. The differences between the two approaches, and their sometimes mutual supportiveness, are illustrated in Table 11.1, which shows different combinations of changes in a company's name, or its **I*Dimension.**

Table 11.1 Name and Identity Change

	New name	Same name
Continuity in the firm's I*Dimension	Cell 1 Altria Veolia	Cell 4 Ikea Bang & Olufsen
Change in the firm's I*Dimension	Cell 3 Danone Vivendi	Cell 2 Nokia 3M

Cell 1 illustrates contexts where top management changed the firm's name without seeking to alter its essence, a process of which Altria is a perfect example. In 2001, following many years of internal discussions about the adverse effects of too close an association of the corporation name with tobacco, health concerns, activist campaigns, and lawsuits, the board of Philip Morris decided to change its corporate name to Altria.[2] Despite the new name, the company maintained its active involvement with tobacco and the production, marketing, and distribution of cigarettes. Its senior management and board apparently hoped that the new name would make it less visibly connected to cigarettes in the minds of external stakeholders.

Veolia, the new name for what had historically been the core businesses of Compagnie Générale des Eaux, is another example of a name change that was unconnected to the essence of the firm. The company, which inherited the traditional businesses spun off by Jean-Marie Messier from CGE under the name Vivendi Environnement, was renamed Veolia to distance itself from the stigma associated with Vivendi and its demise under his leadership.

Companies in Cell 2 went through a very different process in which their identities were deeply altered but their names remained the same. Founded in 1865 as a paper manufacturer, Nokia morphed first into a rubber boots producer, then into a consumer electronics firm, and then, more recently, into a communications company. In the process, Nokia went through successive mergers, acquisitions, and divestments, but its managers at no time felt compelled to change its corporate name. Similar processes occurred in the United States at 3M, GE, and, more recently, IBM.

Cell 3 includes companies in which a name change was part of a change in the firm's *I*Dimension*. The decision, in 1994, to rename BSN after its star brand, Danone, signaled that the evolution from a French glass manufacturer to an international agri-food corporation, initiated by the current CEO's father, Antoine Riboud, in the early 1970s, was complete:

In June 1994, (the management) decided to drop BSN, which seemed to reflect the company's past rather than looking ahead to the future, and adopt the name of The Groupe DANONE, symbolized by a little boy gazing up at a star.[3]

Jean-Marie Messier's decision to rename Compagnie Générale des Eaux illustrates a different approach. In this case, changing the company name at the very outset was part of a radical plan to transform CGE into a global media and communications company.

Finally, Cell 2 contains examples of companies whose deeply rooted identities and external appearances are characterized by remarkable continuity over very long time frames. These companies seem to have found the magic formula of eternal youth and health. At times, these companies were seriously challenged, as Ikea was in the United States or Bang & Olufsen was in the 1980s. They have been able to rebound by leveraging and further asserting their unique identities.[4]

Although organizations such as Ikea and Bang & Olufsen have been able to expand and thrive within their historical identities and names, other organizations, such as IBM and Nokia, could not survive and thrive without altering their deeply rooted sense of themselves. When changing an organization's *I*Dimension* is required, managers can pursue such change in two very different ways. Our research enabled us to distinguish evolutionary and revolutionary change in the *I*Dimension.* The remainder of this chapter discusses each of these modes of change and concludes with an assessment of their respective benefits and pitfalls.

Evolutionary Change in the *I*Dimension*

Our research suggests that this is the most frequent mode of identity change. Many large contemporary firms, including household names such as GE, 3M, Nokia, IBM, Siemens, and Danone, are radically different from who they were in their early years. Unless you are familiar with the history of 3M, for example, you would never know that its name stands for "The Minnesota Mining and Manufacturing Company," which

...was founded in 1902 at the Lake Superior town of Two Harbors, Minn. Five businessmen set out to mine a mineral deposit for grinding-wheel abrasives. But the deposits proved to be of little value, and the new Minnesota Mining and Manufacturing Co. quickly moved to nearby Duluth to focus on sandpaper products.[5]

Interestingly, however, none of the companies just mentioned experienced an abrupt redefinition of their identities. Rather, their new identities evolved gradually through a long series of strategic moves and organizational changes. This gradual process is illustrated well by the case of Danone.

Before becoming known as Danone, BSN was a French glass company whose acronym reflected the merger, in 1966, of two family businesses, Boussois and Souchon Neuvesel. As we noted earlier, the adoption, in 1994, of the name Danone capped two decades of company-transforming acquisitions. No longer involved just in glass manufacturing, BSN became a global food-and-beverage corporation that included Dannon yogurt, Evian mineral water, and Kronenbourg beer.

Antoine Riboud had tried at first to grow the family business into a global manufacturer of all types of glass. But he changed course after his failed hostile takeover of rival Saint Gobain in 1969. Facing the high energy costs and recession of the 1970s, he exited the plate-glass side of the business to protect the glass-bottle side. The rationale for BSN's first acquisitions, in mineral water, beer, and baby food, was to defend the glass-bottle business, threatened by the development of alternative and disposable packaging, by "making the contents for its containers." The most important milestones were the acquisitions of Evian in 1969, Kronenbourg and European Breweries in 1970, Gervais Danone in 1973, Generale Biscuit in 1986, and Nabisco's European business in 1989.

Overall, the transformation of BSN to Danone took more than two decades. As Riboud acknowledged on several occasions, he entered the food and beverage business primarily out of necessity, to defend the historical core business. The new vision of BSN as a food-and-beverage company emerged only after the success of the first diversification steps.

Riboud's legendary prudence allowed him to manage the transformation of BSN cautiously. Because he perceived the creation of new brands as too slow and risky, he consistently diversified through acquisition of established brands. To further minimize risk, Riboud always paid for acquisitions with BSN stock. When he retired, after more than three decades at the helm, he handed his son a company markedly different from the family business he inherited in the late 1950s.

Danone, Nokia, and 3M, among others, have already completed one or several cycles of identity change, and others are morphing right in front of our eyes. Under Steve Jobs, Apple seems to be evolving away from the maverick personal computer company of the early 1980s into a mature, fiercely marketing-driven, high-technology, consumer-oriented company with a "cool" image, a legacy of the early days. As it achieves leadership in the world automotive industry and spreads its operating web across the globe, Toyota is working hard in its usual cautious and methodical way to redefine itself from a Japanese company to a truly global one. And in Europe, Gerard Kleisterlee, the current chairman and CEO of Philips, is significantly, although silently, distancing the company from its identity as a Dutch manufacturer of consumer electronics to a new identity, after several years of acquisitions, primarily in the medical sector, and divestments. The "new" Philips is described on the company Web site[6] as follows:

Royal Philips Electronics of the Netherlands is a global leader in healthcare, lifestyle and technology, delivering products, services and solutions through the brand promise of "sense and simplicity."

Revolutionary Change of the *I*Dimension*

Revolutionary change of identity is fraught with risk, and for this reason it is less common than evolutionary change. The revolutionary process can be likened to a big bang, where a firm is stripped of its old identity and given a new one. The process is swift and unfolds over a very short period of time, and the articulation of the new identity precedes its implementation.

Vivendi and GEC Marconi are good illustrations of revolutionary change of identity and the perils associated with it.

As noted in Chapter 9, Jean-Marie Messier undertook an extensive and rapid restructuring of the old Compagnie Générale des Eaux from a French municipal services company into a global media and communications company. To achieve the transformation and give substance to the new identity, Messier embarked on a rapid string of mergers and acquisitions in the media and entertainment business and divested or spun off businesses that no longer fit with the new identity. It proved exceedingly difficult to integrate these acquisitions, however, and these difficulties were magnified by the bursting of the Internet bubble and subsequent depression of financial markets. Under pressure from a variety of external stakeholders, Vivendi's board fired him in a highly publicized move.[7] A similar process unfolded in the case of the British conglomerate GEC. Immediately upon his appointment as CEO, Lord Simpson initiated a swift transformation of the company, hitherto primarily a defense contractor, from "an industrial age conglomerate into an information age leader." As the *Financial Times* put it:

"GEC had become a slow-moving, Euro-centric, joint venture-bound entity," says Lord Simpson. The "first shaft of light" in the process of changing the company was the decision to focus on telecoms equipment and services. "We had to change the way the company was positioned. We were looking to be in a high growth, high margin, high technology sector—and so telecoms seemed obvious."[8]

To give substance to the new Marconi, over a period of four years Lord Simpson embarked on a spree of divestments of old businesses and acquisitions in the telecom sector. Five years into the process, however, Lord Simpson's vision proved to be seriously flawed. What happened at Marconi was widely viewed as a corporate disaster, in much the same way as Vivendi symbolized management failure in France: "Marconi's continuing decline is one of the most devastating in recent UK corporate history. It is now valued at €375m, compared with €34.5bn at its peak last September."[9]

Revolutionary change of a firm's identity is a risky undertaking, as suggested by the examples of Marconi and Vivendi. Swift identity change may be required, and may be less risky, when two or more companies merge and the new management works swiftly to define a new identity for the combined operations. The merger, in 1999, of Rhone-Poulenc (RP) and Hoechst, the French and German pharmaceutical companies, shows how chief executives can help a newly merged company "forget" the identity of its parents and shape its own character.

Although it took many by surprise, the sudden announcement of the merger was just one more episode in the ongoing consolidation of the global pharmaceutical industry. The merger had the classic rationale: catching up with a rapidly consolidating industry and improving performance through cost synergies and better R&D spending.

In contrast to the DaimlerChrysler merger, in which the German and American operations continued to be managed within the original organizations, RP and Hoechst were blended into Aventis. To ease the creation of the new identity, the former RP and Hoechst leaders made a series of symbolic and substantive decisions. Jürgen Dormann from Hoechst and Jean-René Fourtou from RP shared the executive suite until March 2002, as chairman and vice chairman of the management board. The new, neutral name and new headquarters in Strasbourg, on the French-German border, were designed to make the French and the Germans feel at home. English, neutral in this setting, became the official company language. Dormann and Fourtou also used a consulting company to review the qualifications of 800 French and German managers and to help Aventis hire the best. Meanwhile, they started divesting sidelines, such as animal nutrition and agrochemicals, so as to focus on pharmaceuticals.

The positive reception of the merger by the financial community and the good economic performance of Aventis in the ensuing years suggest that the swift approach to building a new identity was bearing fruit. But the hostile takeover of the company by its French archrival Sanofi-Synthelabo in 2004 does not allow us to draw definitive conclusions about the effectiveness of swift identity engineering in the aftermath of a merger.

The Benefits and Pitfalls of Evolutionary and Revolutionary Change of the *I*Dimension*

The preceding discussion suggested that revolutionary identity change is more risky than gradual transformation. Attempting to introduce abrupt identity change increases the vulnerability of the organization in that time bracket where it is no longer who it used to be and is not yet who its leadership wants people, internally and externally, to believe it is becoming. In this transition period, there will always be some stakeholders who watch the big bang with a dose of skepticism, and others who may be directly threatened by the course of events. Also, as the old organizational structures and routines are dismantled and replaced by new ones, it is normal for the quality of operations to suffer. In such a context, it takes only a little bad news to spread and sustain doubt about the soundness of the chief executive's plan.

By contrast, evolutionary change, because it does not alter all of an organization's identity anchors at the same time, communicates an impression of continuity even while the organization is undergoing far-reaching change. Here, the chief executive does not have to be explicit about his or her intent to change the firm's identity and thus does not run the risk of sudden opposition from influential stakeholders—internal or external. As in the case of Danone, the chief executive might not have a grand plan at the outset. The evolutionary approach also minimizes the chances of sudden deterioration of the firm's performance, and the leadership team can plant the seeds of the new identity while continuing to reap the benefits of the old identity for some time.

Although our arguments are clearly biased in favor of evolutionary change, managers should make their choice between the two approaches in full awareness of the time frame. Evolutionary change in identity is less risky, but it requires years, sometimes decades, to be completed. However, the increasing pace of economic, political, social, regulatory, and technological change puts the leaders of today's organizations under pressure for swift operational and strategic results, and this pressure may not give them the luxury of the time required for thorough identity reengineering.

The Levers for Identity Change

To produce gradual or revolutionary change in the *I*Dimension,* managers can use the same kinds of symbolic or substantive levers available for reinforcing an organization's identity.

Managers can seek to alter internal and external beliefs about the essence of their firm by producing a new discourse that is critical of the current identity or that promotes an alternative view of the firm. The new identity can be served by rewriting a corporate history that shows continuity between some forgotten aspect of the firm's past and the identity being promoted. Managers can also convey the new identity through a new name or logo, an indoctrination program for current and future employees, or collective events of various sorts.

Substantive levers of identity change are decisions about the firm's more tangible dimensions. These include strategic decisions that drive the firm away from its historical roots and toward a new life, recruitment of key personnel who bring along different values and can help change how the organization thinks of itself, and rather mundane operating decisions that can contribute to shaping core beliefs about the organization. Among all substantive levers, however, the choice of the chief executive has the highest potential impact on a firm's identity.

Common Ingredients of Successful Identity Change

Our investigation of many cases has enabled us to identify five ingredients for successful identity change:

1. Vision. In all the successful transformations that we examined, the leaders could see clearly—often before others—that a deeply rooted identity that served the firm well could become a serious liability. They could articulate a vision of the changes needed to seize the new opportunities and preempt the threats facing their firms.

2. Effective communication. Successful identity architects can create simple and easy-to-communicate messages about the need to change and the direction in which they are driving the organization. More importantly, these leaders have no problem repeating the same ideas and messages until they are internalized by the key stakeholders. They do not satisfy themselves with formal communication channels to get their message across. Instead, they throw their persona in the arena and deliver their messages to audiences in various meetings and speaking occasions.

3. Consistency. Effective identity architects gain credibility, internally and externally, by aligning their daily decisions and verbal behavior with the vision they articulate for the company. By so doing, they show that the new identity constitutes an effective framework for dealing with business issues and encourage others to do the same.

4. Leadership continuity. As the many examples discussed throughout the book show, changing a firm's identity requires years—and, in extreme cases, decades. Continuity in leadership is necessary if the identity of a large and well-established company is to be successfully altered.

5. Luck and positive signals. These are needed by leaders who undertake an ambitious change of the firm's identity. No matter how necessary or attractive a new identity may be, if the firm experiences severe performance problems in the middle of a metamorphosis, the process may well be stillborn or aborted.

Endnotes

1. *Business Week*, June 11, 2007: "At 3M, a Struggle Between Efficiency and Creativity: How CEO George Buckley Is Managing the Yin and Yang of Discipline and Imagination."

2. For more background on the circumstances of and reactions to the name change, see Smith, Elizabeth A., and Ruth E. Malone. 2003. "Altria Means Tobacco: Philip Morris's Identity Crisis." *American Journal of Public Health,* 93(4): 553–556.

3. www.danone.com, accessed November 8, 2006.

4. Ravasi, D., and M. Schultz, 2006. "Responding to Organizational Identity Threats: Exploring the Role of Organizational Culture." *Academy of Management Journal,* 49(3): 433–458.

5. www.3M.com, accessed November 8, 2006.

6. www.philips.com, accessed November 8, 2006.

7. The circumstances of Messier's ousting are summarized in Chapter 4.

8. *Financial Times,* March 15, 2000: "A Familiar Name Is Reborn as Group Transforms Itself."

9. *Financial Times,* October 3, 2001: "Lord Weinstock's Baby: In the Pits or on the Skids?"

epilogue

At the end of this journey into the *I*Dimension*, we would like to emphasize the key ideas developed throughout the book and pursue their implications for business leaders in the Age of Identity.

The dominant business paradigm today is grounded in a view of the firm as a rational economic agent that should take advantage of opportunities wherever they are found and shed activities that are unprofitable. This view puts a premium on economic calculation and financial engineering. Implicit in this paradigm is the notion that the perfectly rational firm can break with its past and erase its memory when these hinder its ability to create economic value. Also inherent in the paradigm is a conception of firms as commodities that can, and must be, bought, sold, merged, and de-merged at will when the interests of their shareowners so dictate. This view, however, ignores the fact that firms are human organizations with enduring identities. This view also fails to take into account the impact of identity issues at every level of human organization—starting with crises and new possibilities of identity choice at individual and organizational levels, and extending to threats of clashes at the level of whole civilizations.

The principal theme of this book is that leaders in the Age of Identity need to go beyond the usual strategic, operational, and financial calculations used to define priorities and guide decisions and appreciate the influence of the *I*Dimension* on the performance of their companies. The examples we have presented throughout the book demonstrate that even the most highly regarded executives—individuals widely considered among the best and brightest in the world of business—can run into serious trouble if they rely too much on their traditional professional management toolbox. In these examples, otherwise-talented leaders were blindsided by identity issues they neither anticipated nor knew how to cope with.

Throughout the book, we have sought to demonstrate that the very identity that was an extremely valuable asset at one point in a company's history can become a significant liability at another point. Part of effective leadership is recognizing when it is one or the other and knowing how to respond. When you sense that the liabilities of an identity outweigh its benefits, you should not shrink from attempting to change it.

To help you diagnose and lead with the *I*Dimension,* we developed an identity audit methodology and a number of frameworks for use in making choices about identity mergers and acquisitions, spin-offs, strategic alliances, and firms exploiting a portfolio of brands that have their own identities in the marketplace. In each of these contexts, you basically are confronted with two generic questions.

First, how much convergence is there, both internally and externally, regarding the *I*Dimension*? Recall that the managerial challenges are significantly different when there is convergence both internally and externally as opposed to when there is divergence in both. And the challenges are different still when there is convergence in one but not the other. When there is convergence in the inside and outside view of our firm, we and the outside world both have to agree on who we are. When there is divergence in both views, neither we nor the outside world can agree on who we are. In some cases, we can have a high level of agreement on who we are, but the outside world does not hold a coherent view of us. In still others, we're not sure who we are, but the outside world is sure. You need to know which of these four possible scenarios best describes the situation your firm faces.

The second question is whether you should draw on your firm's existing identity to guide key decisions. Or should you undertake identity change so that decisions that are inconsistent with the current identity envelope become possible and desirable within a redefined identity?

A firm's identity can be changed. But it cannot be changed by fiat. Changing the identity of an organization takes more than a new mission statement, a new name, or a new visual identity. Identity change is complete only when a critical mass of insiders and outsiders recognize and validate what is new. The new identity must be widely endorsed, and this implies that leaders must be salespeople, shaping perceptions and rallying coalitions around their proposals. To nurture competent leaders for the Age of Identity, management training and development initiatives need to put even more emphasis on psychological, communication, and political skills.

As much as such training is necessary and useful for CEOs and senior managers, it is also necessary for boards of directors. Given the impact of the chief executive and top management team on an organization, an effective board of directors must include identity awareness among the criteria it uses in selecting a new chief executive officer. Particularly when board members believe that the firm's current identity is problematic, it is important to select a person for the top position whose background and experience in leading change demonstrate an appreciation and understanding of the significance of identity and who, like Carlos Ghosn, will challenge the status quo while respecting the firm's soul.

Finally, if you are contemplating a move from one firm to another, you should consider the degree of fit between your own self-concept and the identity of the firm you are thinking about joining. No matter how attractive the job or the package, if you are at odds with the soul of a corporation, and if you are unwilling or unable to close that gap in one direction or the other, you are stacking the odds of success against yourself. Peter Drucker had it right when he reminded us that, at the end of the day, managing others begins with managing oneself.

Index

In five days, even Darwin would be shocked at how you've changed.

WHARTON EXECUTIVE EDUCATION | **We're all business.®**

Evolve and learn at Wharton. Introducing the Wharton Learning Continuum. From the pre-program coursework to the post-program follow up, it will transform your career. Request your information kit at **execed@wharton.upenn.edu**, or visit our website at **executiveeducation.wharton.upenn.edu**. Call **800.255.3932** (U.S. or Canada) or **+1.215.898.1776** (worldwide).

Wharton
UNIVERSITY *of* PENNSYLVANIA

What's Your Story?
Storytelling to Move Markets, Audiences, People, and Brands

RYAN MATHEWS AND WATTS WACKER

Storytelling is the universal human activity. Every society, at every stage of history, has told stories—and listened to them intently, passionately. Stories are how people tell each other who they are, where they came from, how they're unique, what they believe. Stories capture their memories of the past and their hopes for the future. Stories are one more thing, too: They are your most powerful, most underutilized tool for competitive advantage. Whether you know it or not, your business is already telling stories. *What's Your Story?* will help you take control of those stories and make them work for you. Legendary business thinkers Ryan Mathews and Watts Wacker reveal how to craft an unforgettable story…create the back story that makes it believable…make sure your story cuts through today's relentless bombardment of consumer messages…and gets heard, remembered, and acted on.

ISBN 9780132277426, © 2008, 240 pp., $24.99 USA, $28.99 CAN

The Advantage-Makers
How Exceptional Leaders Win by Creating Opportunities Others Don't

STEVEN FEINBERG

Some leaders consistently see possibilities others miss. They learn more, learn faster, and transform their insights into breakaway strategies. They are more effective collaborators, more powerful influencers, better at handling adversity, and dramatically more successful at execution. They are the Advantage-Makers. Their winning skills are not innate: they are entirely teachable and learnable. Steven Feinberg has been teaching these skills to executives for more than twenty years: leaders who've gone on to transform their organizations.

Feinberg helps you to master every skill Advantage-Makers need. He doesn't just exhort you to "think different," he shows you how. You'll learn how to find the "commanding vantage point" in your situation, no matter how complex or dynamic… and use your high ground to spot and maximize every opportunity.

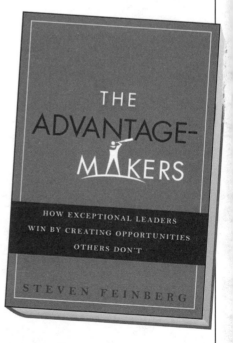

ISBN 9780132347785, © 2008, 304 pp., $27.99 USA, $31.99 CAN